bent street 4.1
love from a distance

intimacy and technology in time of COVID-19

Bent Street: Australian LGBTIQA+ Art, Writing & Ideas
Edited by:

Jennifer Power
Henry von Doussa
Timothy W. Jones

Series Editor-in-Chief: Tiffany Jones

Clouds of Magellan Press | Melbourne

Bent Street: Australian LGBTIQA+ Art, Writing & Ideas is published twice yearly by Clouds of Magellan Press, Melbourne.

www.cloudsofmagellanpress.net

Bent Street publishes a midyear themed edition with guest editors; and an open-themed end-of-year edition. *Bent Street* welcomes contributions at any time from the Australian and international LGBTIQA+ community. Visit bentstreet.net for submission details.

ISSN 2652-6581 (Online)
ISSN 2652-659X (Print)

ISBN: (paperback) 978-0-6487469-3-5
ISBN: (ebook) 978-0-6487469-4-2

Series Editor-in-Chief: Tiffany Jones
Contributing Editors: Ashley Sievwright, Gordon Thompson
Editors for *Bent Street 4.1*: Jennifer Power, Henry von Doussa, Timothy W. Jones

Logo: Andrew Liu
Design: Gordon Thompson

Publication and distribution, Lightning Source, through eBook Alchemy.
ebookalchemy.com

Cover: *time to get my life together*—Jake Cruz

Acknowledgment

In the spirit of reconciliation *Bent Street* acknowledges the Traditional Custodians of country throughout Australia and their connections to land, sea and community. We pay our respect to their Elders past, present and emerging, and extend that respect to all Aboriginal and Torres Strait Islander peoples reading this journal.

Indigenous walk – Woodlands Historic Park, July 2020 – G Thompson

contents

FOREWORD

Since 2017, the year of Marriage Equality, we have produced three editions of *Bent Street,* a journal variously described as 'a twisted tapestry of our time', 'the road less travelled', and 'a page for rainbow essayists, yarn spinners and queer theorists, a canvas for diverse doodlers and alternative artists, an ear for wrathful rants and interesting interviews, an eye for raw reflections and a mouth for personal opinions'.

Bent Street is now evolving to become a bi-annual publication, with our usual end-of-year edition (The Year in Queer), and now a mid-year edition plugging into different topical areas. We are thrilled to welcome Jennifer Power, Henry von Doussa, and Timothy W. Jones as our Guest Editors for this first special edition on Intimacy and Technology, seen through the frame of COVID-19. The circumstances of social distancing and the move to mostly online contact for many Australian alternative and artistic communities are partly what prompted our new publishing model. We see it as a way of keeping a community electricity alight and boosting our connectivity.

We would like to thank the Australian Research Centre in Sex, Health and Society (ARCSHS) and La Trobe University Transforming Human Societies Research Focus Area for their support for this issue. We thank all of our contributors and welcome new writers and creatives to these pages, as well as familiar names. We hope that the *Bent Street* model of creative collision will continue to spark possibilities through fusing together our many disparate ideas and energies.

Tiffany Jones—Editor-in-Chief, *Bent Street*
Gordon Thompson—Publisher, *Clouds of Magellan Press*

Park exercise equipment, May 2020—G Thompson

INTRODUCTION

The rise of the internet and digital technology has facilitated a new world of human connection. Never has it been so easy for people to speak across continents and timezones. Never has it been so commonplace for people to connect, often in quite intimate terms, with strangers. Phones, apps and chat rooms have facilitated new cultures of sex, dating and romance. Sex is instantly available online. Bodies are available. Love is available.

Arguably, queers were the great early adapters of digital dating. Grindr led the way on geo-locating hook up apps, extending the span of gay men's sexual cultures across digital and physical space. Meanwhile the internet has enhanced queers' opportunities to find their people, explore queer life and seek affirmation: perhaps before venturing into queer physical spaces, or at times when those spaces are not available.

In recent months, social lockdowns imposed by COVID-19 have made the role that new technologies play in human connection starkly obvious. In lockdown, most of us are living an ever larger part of our lives through Zoom and Facetime. People communicate more often, and more intensely, though instant text messaging. Tech and human intimacy have become more palpably entwined than ever.

However, while digital communication may now be the most conspicuous form of technology facilitating and mediating human intimacy, technology has always been a collaborator in human relations – particularly when it comes to sex and intimacy. It is not only a smartphone, computer, or a new app that links people or shapes the nature of human connection. Often human attachments are produced in conjunction with much more mundane and quotidian technologies – coffee, alcohol, the kitchen table, the design of a sofa, the layout of a restaurant, the bus that drives us across town, the ring we wear on our finger.

Our aim for *Bent Street 4.1* is to cast a broad lens on the role of technologies in shaping human intimacy with a nod to the impact of COVID-19. We asked people to reflect broadly on the role that technologies, both old and new, play in mediating human intimacy and shaping queer culture. The contributions we present in this issue do, indeed, show how technologies both constitute and are constituted by relational intimacies: what, as Lauren Berlant has said, are in reality, 'the kinds of connections that impact on people, and on which they depend for living (if not "a life")'. Many of the first-person accounts, the theoretical engagements and the visual arts in this issue, are articulations of technologies as ways out of isolation, ways of finding—or recognising—your crew and enacting belonging. The viewing of pornography for the first time on a Super 8 film among peers; the joining of two cans with string as a visual reminded that even as children we know technology can be playful and desire to mimic its connective potential; the medical technologies of the body that transform lives; the rise of sexbots and artificial intelligence in providing comfort; the excitement of building a new relationship via text message; and the use of GPS technologies in the delicate undulations of power in the dominance/submission relations of BDSM are all testament to the transformative potential of technology and desire in human becoming.

Jennifer Power, Henry von Doussa, Timothy W. Jones
July 2020

INTERVIEWS

10 bent street 4.1

INTERVIEWS
SUZANNE FRASER
AMANDA GESSELMAN
JAMIE HAKIM

Following are edited transcripts of interviews with leading researchers in fields relating to gender, sexuality, intimacy and technologies. The interviews were conducted by Jennifer Power in the leadup to a seminar held at La Trobe University titled 'Love from a Distance: Intimacy and Technology'. The theme for this seminar was inspired by the COVID-19 pandemic in which social lockdowns and quarantine forced more people to rely on digital media to seek or maintain intimate connections.

COVID-19 has brought to the forefront the way that technology plays a central role in mediating human intimate relationships. While this is most obvious when it comes to communication technologies, other technologies also facilitate and shape the ways in which we connect and relate to other people—particularly when it comes to sex and intimacy. Historically, bicycles, for example, have been credited with introducing sweeping changes to marriage trends in Western countries, as they gave people capacity to travel further and mingle in more diverse social circles. The design of physical spaces—houses, bedrooms, neighbourhoods, offices, cafes, bars—moderate the ways we interact with the people around us. Reflecting on the form and function of a broad range of technologies, and the way that they are adopted into human action and experiences, helps us to make sense of how intimacy can be facilitated through a 'collaboration' between humans and non-humans (machines, devices, objects).

INTIMACY AND UNEXPECTED TECHNOLOGIES
SUZANNE FRASER

Professor Suzanne Fraser is Director of the Australian Research Centre in Sex, Health and Society (ARCSHS) at La Trobe University. She is also visiting Professorial Fellow at the Centre for Social Research in Health at the University of New South Wales. Suzanne's PhD is in Gender Studies, and her research focuses on the body, gender, health and the self. Suzanne is the author of a number of books on the body and health in society and culture. Her most recent book is entitled *Habits: Remaking addiction*, co-authored with David Moore and Helen Keane, and her previous works cover a range of topics including cosmetic surgery, methadone maintenance treatment, the politics of hepatitis C and the politics of addiction.

Over the last few years, Suzanne's research has focused on two Australian Research Council-funded studies, one exploring injecting practices and harm reduction needs among men who inject performance and image enhancing drugs, and the other investigating impediments to the uptake and diffusion in Australia of take-home naloxone, the opioid overdose medication known to save lives. Professor Fraser's recent work has focused in part on technologies associated with injecting drug use. In this interview she talks about the ways in which technologies that respond to opioid overdose or support safer injecting can offer a resource for thinking about how 'objects' and 'technologies' are implicated in the shaping of human intimacy.

Jennifer Power (JP): Can you tell me a bit about your work as it relates to themes of technology and intimacy?

Suzanne Fraser (SF): Over the years I've been intensely interested in the relationship between selves, bodies, technologies and society. My early studies in Women's Studies and then Gender Studies brought up time and again knotty questions about how we should understand individuals, subjectivity, power and structures, and prompted me repeatedly to interrogate taken-for-granted binaries such as nature/culture, self/other, purity/pollution and masculinity/femininity. Part of that process of interrogation involved rethinking go-to objections to social developments such as the rise of cosmetic surgery in the 1980s and 1990s (the subject of my PhD thesis). At that time it wasn't uncommon for feminists to criticise cosmetic surgery as an unnatural intervention into women's bodies. While perhaps an understandable reaction, I perceived it to be self-defeating in that discourses of nature were also part of the logics delimiting women's choices. When Donna Haraway pointed out that technological innovation, and its influence on daily life, was not something we could simply stop or abandon, and instead must think through more carefully, I found this extremely productive. She rejected simplistic and potentially counterproductive assumptions about pure, pre-technological bodies, and in a moment of hyperbole appreciated by many feminists, declared she would rather be a cyborg than a goddess.

All that might seem a long way from the question I'm answering here, but for me it isn't. Technologies are part of who we are: they can help shape our lives including our forms of intimacy. That said, how this relationship works is also worthy of close consideration. As Bruno Latour has noted, technologies aren't just passive, neutral tools that can be deployed to fulfil our goals. Nor are they governing devices that dictate use and outcomes. Instead they create what he calls 'affordances'—opportunities and tendencies. I observed this at work in the uses to which cosmetic surgery procedures were put, and the discourses that circulated through them. Later, when I started to work on other issues such as sexuality, blood-borne virus prevention and drug use, similar dynamics also became clear to me. In all these contexts I see similar issues in play relating to technology and intimacy. Contemporary life offers an array of technological means of reaching for and enjoying intimacy. Those means are also routinely deployed for ends that would seem not to have been intended or predicted by the makers, and which might diminish intimacy, at least for some. In the process, the very terms of the engagement come to be redefined—the nature of intimacy, for example, is no doubt undergoing change in response to the advent of social media, particularly under pandemic-related quarantine conditions. So, for me, the multidirectional, unpredictable, yet not entirely unmoored relationship between technology and intimacy forms a thread that runs through all my work.

JP: When we recently spoke about this topic you gave the example of the work you have done that involved designing a 'fitpack' for couples. You used the term (I think) 'unexpected technologies of intimacy'. Can you describe that example here?

[Note. A fitpack is a small container that holds a supply of clean hypodermic syringes, swabs and a container for safe disposal of syringes]

SF: The work my colleagues and I have done looking at drug use-related technologies might offer resources for thinking about intimacy and technology. Two pieces of work come to mind as especially relevant here. One discusses the use of the overdose-reversal medication naloxone within an intimate relationship to afford care for a person with a terminal illness. In the other, the safe injecting fitpack is the focus, with the design of the fitpack understood as materialising a particular approach to intimacy. While conventional fitpacks are designed for individuals, explicitly materialising the responsibility of the individual in preventing the transmission of blood-borne viruses, a new model developed by our research team was designed around couples who inject together, acknowledging their intimate relationships, easing equipment management, and supporting discussions about transmission prevention.

JP: Are there any questions relating to technology and intimacy or technology and sexuality do you find yourself thinking or wondering about?

SF: Perhaps because my own working life has been so affected by COVID-19 recently, and remote working relationships have become my primary way of engaging with other people, I've found myself thinking about the affordances of Zoom and other electronic meeting technologies. It might be that we rarely think of workplace interactions as forms of intimacy, but in an odd way, perhaps because Zoom has put my colleagues' faces and voices right in front of me, I feel a particular kind of social intimacy has emerged, at least from my perspective. It might be I'm alone in this perception, but if not, I have wondered how it might shape workplace relationships and even decision-making and outcomes. More broadly, if such meeting styles continue after quarantine, I've wondered whether it will have an impact on the capacity for people living with disabilities to participate more easily in public life and at least some occupations, and whether that will afford new social intimacies among people who otherwise rarely engage with each other, and even over time reshape industries, policies and institutions. And of course, while I've just used the word 'disability', this is a heavily freighted and contested word. Certainly, if electronic meetings and working from home were normalised as a result of the pandemic, a wholly different landscape of so-called disability might emerge. Some people previously excluded from face-to-face meetings by mobility or other issues, for example, might be newly able to participate fully. In turn, greater clarity around the sources of exclusion—institutional, social or political rather than individual—might be afforded.

To turn to a very different subject and context, I don't suppose any of us will quickly forget the terrible and shocking intimacy in which we became enfolded when footage of the killing of George Floyd in the US emerged as a result of smartphone camera technology. While such cameras have been used to create and circulate painful and denigrating images, they have also been used to share images of desperate urgency and importance, images that may change society and governance in positive ways. Rendering the treatment of George Floyd right into our hands, homes and thoughts via a device that may for many be our most intimate possession, with the voices of those begging for his life right in our ears, was an agonising production of intimacy that I hope changes our world forever.

Phone Sex—Henry von Doussa

INTIMACY, TECHNOLOGY AND EMOJIS
AMANDA GESSELMAN

Amanda Gesselman PhD is a social psychologist at the Kinsey Institute and the inaugural Anita Aldrich Endowed Research Scientist at Indiana University. Dr. Gesselman's research examines dating and sexuality of single adults, with an emphasis on technology and health behaviors; the psychology, sexuality, and health of romantic couples; and the intersection of human development, stigma, and sexuality.

Jennifer Power (JP): Can you tell us a bit about your work as it relates to themes of technology and intimacy?

Amanda Gesselman (AG): I study new trends in people's love and sex lives, and how they impact connection and well-being. In today's world, these emerging trends almost always include technology, so I study how technology can be a conduit for meaningful connection. My recent work has included a study of 141,000 women from 190 countries around the world on how they've used technology in their sexual lives. My collaborators and I found that over half the sample had engaged in sexting, and this was relatively consistent across major world regions. Twenty percent of women around the world were also using apps to learn more about sex and sexual intimacy, which really emphasizes how linked technology and intimacy are in our world today.

My colleagues and I are currently working on an ongoing study of intimate connection in digital spaces, with a specific focus on adult entertainment cam-sites, where paying visitors can view and interact with a cam model in real time. Although these are marketed as and thought of as purely sexual spaces, a considerable proportion of these visitors don't engage in explicitly sexual interactions or request nudity—one in three feel a personal connection with a model, and many of these visitors report feelings of social support, reduced loneliness, and an equal amount of emotional and sexual gratification.

Last, my colleagues and I are also working on another ongoing study of love and sex in the time of COVID-19. We have a large international sample that we've surveyed in four waves starting in March 2020, when lockdown recommendations first began in the United States. Our preliminary results have shown strong evidence that in 'lockdown', people are heavily relying on technology to create intimate interactions and maintain their intimate relationships.

JP: Human intimacy is often thought of as entirely human—something that exists between people involving emotional and/or physical contact. How should we imagine technology within this?

AG: In my work, I see technology as both bridge and a shapeable tool. I conceptualize technology as the piece that can work to bridge the gap and strengthen a relationship between two people, and also as a tool that we can—with work and some stumbling—figure out how to shape into something that facilitates our human needs. For instance, now that we have the technological capability to find romantic and sexual partners using technology, we have to figure out how to *connect* with them in that same space where there aren't any of the usual visual cues of attraction and compatibility. In my work on emojis, my collaborators and I found that people who used emojis more frequently with potential partners also went on more dates and had more sex over the past year. More frequent use of emojis was associated with personality characteristics like emotional intelligence and more secure attachment, both of which tend to be implicated as characteristics of good quality relationship partners. So these people, likely unknowingly, may have found a way to successfully advertise their traits in a single character and build chemistry with potential partners in ways that people who didn't have those traits did not do.

JP: There is a common perception that technology is playing an increasing role in human relationships due to new digital technologies (mobile phones, mobile cameras, dating apps and so forth). Do you think this is the case? If so, what are the most significant changes that may have occurred as a result of this?

AG: I do. I think the most significant changes that technology has ushered forth in our relationships are the ability to connect with people over long distances, the ability to be in contact frequently, and the ability to harness it for sexual gratification. Not too many generations ago, we met our long-term partners within a few blocks of our family home. Being able to span distances and be exposed to people that you may have never encountered otherwise is very valuable, I think, for finding someone you'd really like to spend your time with, who you're really attracted to, and who is really compatible with you. It also has value in expanding our minds, introducing us to different people and practices. And it can provide more of a safe space to start meeting people before potentially putting your life on the line with an in-person meet-up.

The ability to be in contact immediately, frequently, and privately has surely helped to create and maintain emotionally close relationships. Think of couples who, decades ago, had to endure one going off to war, or off on a months-long sailing trip, or even today's couples who may be subject to stigma and discrimination if they're seen together in public. Technology has provided a way for those people to keep in touch with their support system while being physically separated.

And I think that the role technology is now playing in sex is hard to ignore. Technology and the internet have created a space for any sexual interest to be shared and discussed, and have created methods for engaging sexually without having to, or having the opportunity to, give someone access to your physical body.

JP: What questions relating to technology and intimacy or technology and sexuality do you find yourself thinking or wondering about?

AG: I wonder what long-term changes we would see if human-looking sex robots became widespread and affordable. I wonder what the next generations will come up with to serve their romantic and sexual needs. I wonder if future generations of older people will be less lonely because they're used to interacting through technology and may have an easier time staying connected through those means.

JP: Do you think that the COVID-19 social lockdown periods are likely to have changed the way people use technology to create intimacy with other people? Do you think such changes will have any lasting effects on cultures of sex or intimacy?

AG: I do, and I have some evidence of it in the study my colleagues and I are doing on sex and relationships in the time of COVID-19. We've seen that people—and especially people who are single and who are lonelier—are turning more toward technology to connect with other people. This includes sexual digital behavior, as well. People reported engaging in more sexting and sexually explicit video-chatting, and some subgroups of people are reporting signing up for and using online dating services more. I think the pandemic has changed how we're able to connect, but hasn't changed the need to, so we're seeing people adapt to their current means.

DIGITAL INTIMACY, GENDER AND SEXUALITY
JAMIE HAKIM

Dr Jamie Hakim is a lecturer in Media Studies at the University of East Anglia, where he has been since 2014. His research interests lie at the intersection of digital media, intimacy, embodiment, gender and sexuality. He explores these themes in his book *Work That Body: Male Bodies in Digital Culture* (Rowman & Littlefield International, 2019). The book explores the recent rise of different types of men using digital media to sexualise their bodies, arguing they do this as a way of negotiating living through post-2008 neoliberalism. Dr. Hakim is the principal investigator on the Economic and Social Research Council (ESRC) funded 'Digital Intimacies: how gay and bisexual men use their smartphones to negotiate their cultures of intimacy'.

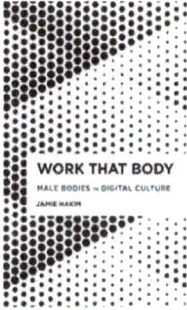

Jennifer Power (JP): Thanks for speaking to me Jamie, can you tell me a little bit about yourself and the work you've been doing lately?

Jamie Hakim (JH): Mostly I do research around digital media, questions of embodiment, questions of intimacy, and recently questions of care. I've got a book out at the moment, called *Work That Body: Male Bodies in Digital Culture,* that looks at the way that over the last decade more men have been using digital media to sexualise their bodies. The argument that I make is that this has happened in relation to a certain set of historical conditions brought about by the 2007/2008 economic crash. So, in the UK particularly, the austerity context has meant men have not been able to rely on the forms of value creation that they once used to. So, they have been sharing images of their sexualised bodies to feel valuable instead. Currently, I'm leading a project called 'Digital Intimacies: how gay and bisexual men use their smart phones to negotiate their cultures of intimacy'. We are taking a similar approach to the one I took in the book, looking at the kind of cultures that have developed around smart phone use, and trying to understand this within political, cultural, social and economic contexts. Over the next six months we are going to be interviewing gay and bisexual men in Scotland and in London about this.

JP: Are you including the full function of smart phones in this? Such as cameras and images as well as use of the apps?

JH: Yes. It felt to me that there is a tendency within some of the work on hook up apps and gay men to imagine that gay men only use the apps to negotiate casual sex. Although we are interested in casual sex, we're also interested in a more capacious understanding of intimacy. So, we'll be looking at different social media platforms, the phone itself, the camera, all sorts of things. We're going to try and get a more holistic understanding of smart phone use, and in a way that tries to capture more about gay men's sexual lives than casual sex, however important that might be to certain gay men. We haven't started doing fieldwork yet, so a lot of our thinking is hypothetical at the moment.

JP: Can you tell us more about how you approach the concept of technology and intimacy in your work?

JH: In the 1960s and 70s, at the beginning of British cultural studies, there was a certain type of critique that argued that you need to understand technology in the context of its wider 'conjunctural' relations, namely in relation to the political, the economic, the social and so on; and that these things are continuously interacting with each other. I'm not sure that it's especially fashionable anymore to use any sort of technological deterministic approach to technology, but this is a particular way out of that. We're using this cultural studies approach to understand the technology as one part of a range of forces that are assembled in a certain way at a particular moment in time. We decentre technology slightly and try to understand its relation to what is happening now economically, politically, culturally, socially, institutionally, and so on—as one piece of the puzzle. When we started the project we obviously hadn't anticipated there would be a global pandemic that would have such enormous political, economic and social consequences!

JP: COVID 19 might end up revealing a lot about people's relationship with technology in their intimate lives, do you think?

JH: Yeah, I think, as your question suggests, there's a real focus now on the way that technologies like smartphones and video conferencing platforms are being used to replace physical intimacy at this moment of social distancing. We're definitely interested in looking at that. But we're also interested in looking at the political, social and economic crises that the pandemic has precipitated in the UK (and globally) and what gay men's place within these crises might end up being. So we're looking at those things at the same time.

JP: It seems there has been a moral positioning of individual behaviours in terms of public health and social distancing in relation to COVID-19. People are called out as irresponsible if they see non cohabiting sexual partners and so forth. There is something in this that is reminiscent of some of the judgement of gay men's sex lives in response to HIV. Public health enables moral scrutiny of people's sexual and intimate lives. Do you agree?

JH: Absolutely. And something else that I've been thinking about is the reduction of the publicness of a gay cultures of intimacy during the pandemic. I mean, think about community spaces—community centres, bookshops, bars, clubs, sex on premises venues, outdoor spaces— obviously what's happened as a result of COVID is the absolute retraction to the private sphere. This might work for some gay men in the age of gay marriage and homonormative domesticity, but it completely erodes the other kinds of spaces that gay men have historically relied on for intimate connection.

JP: I think you have written about that trend toward the privatisation of gay men's intimacy before. Can you talk a bit about that?

JH: I have written about privatisation and gentrification of urban space, and what that has meant for gay men's cultures of intimacy. I need to think about that more in relation to what's happening now. I understand social distancing as a public health issue, where there has been an urgent need to lock down and keep people safe. I do understand that. But there are implications that it has had for gay culture that I think we need to think very carefully about. To be clear, I am not arguing against lockdowns as necessary measures to contain the spread of coronavirus. I am saying that we need to think intersectionally about the retraction of society to the private sphere and what it has meant for different social groups—gay men included.

JP: Human intimacy is often thought of as entirely human, something that exists between two people, whether that's physical or emotional. Given this, how would you explain where technology sits within this dynamic?

JH: There are certain kind of critical perspectives that are being used at the moment that can help make sense of this question. Science and technology studies and 'actor network theory' in particular describe non-human objects like technology as having a degree of agency. Another way of putting it is that agency is distributed across assemblages of humans and non-humans. This is a perspective I admire and find very useful, although don't draw from it much in my work. The concept of intimacy that I am working with at the moment comes from Lauren Berlant. She describes intimacy as the attachments that we depend on for living. This opens a far more capacious understanding of what intimacy is beyond the common sense understanding of intimacy as the private thoughts or feelings two people share. I think questions about the human and the non-human were not in the forefront of critical theory at the time Berlant wrote this, but you can see how it moves us beyond the human. She did write about fetishistic attachments to objects—sexual fetishes—but of course we can develop life-sustaining attachments to technology. We did a focus group a few weeks ago with five gay and bisexual guys in London and what became apparent was that the phone itself was absolutely central to their intimate lives. They actually had an emotional investment in the technology, because it was so crucial to the way that it mediated their human relations, and as a result they had absolutely become very invested in it as an object. There was this great quote from one participant who said: "I wonder when [Alexander Graeme Bell] invented the telephone if he realised that we'd end up investing so much emotions in this piece of technology."

JP: I think anyone who's had a long-distance relationship would concur as well with that. The phone becomes so central to that everyday connection. There can be anxiety if the phone's not with you.

JH: Yeah, the participants talked about that. They also talked about the way blue ticks on Whatsapp dominated their life, especially the investment in the blue ticks. The blue ticks show someone has read their message, so they know and then wonder why they haven't got back to them, or why hadn't they read it. I mean this wasn't incidental, it was very much part of it. The phone and the blue ticks became ways of mediating their relationships. They also talked about what we've called purely mediated intimacy, so for example the relationship they have with porn stars and so forth.

JP: So, imagined relationships or actual interactions?

Imagined relationships. So there's this whole kind of continuously shifting terrain of technologically mediated intimacy in which people and technology are, using a word which I think is useful from post-humanism, 'entangled'. These things are entangled: they're separate, but they are deeply entangled—like spaghetti you can see the strands are separate but they're impossible to delineate. I think that is a useful image to describe the ways that the human and technological relate, certainly now with digital media.

JP: That makes a lot of sense to me. Even just to go back to that long-distance relationship example, if you had a lover in different city or country 20 years ago you couldn't have maintained the constant connection in the way that you can now with phones. So technology is neutral in that sense, it shapes what's possible and becomes entangled in that relationship.

JH: Exactly. I 100% agree with you. Did you see [the television series] Normal People? There is a scene where the two main characters are watching each other sleep using Skype.

JP: That's my favourite scene, I've thought about that many times when talking to people about tech and intimacy. I never imagined Skype could be so intimate. Or at least the scene was filmed in a way that made it seem intimate.

JH: Yeah and as I'm talking, I think I realise we're talking against a more common-sense idea that technology interrupts intimacy or is inauthentic intimacy. But then people's experience is not necessarily this. It came up in the focus group—there was definitely a sense that meeting in bars is much better than meeting on Grindr because a Grindr meet was always somehow inauthentic. But later on the participants were saying things that completely contradicted this and that their intimate lives absolutely depended on apps like Grindr and their smartphones more generally.

JP: I agree, I hear a lot in kind of contemporary discourse or discourse on technology about it being an inauthentic or a stilted form of intimacy. But I have also heard some people speak about the way technology opens intimacy or gives people confidence to say more or be more vulnerable because it is often communication that is at a distance but also quite spontaneous—like texting or messaging. Has that come up in your work?

JH: That's a really interesting question. Well I mean, one of the examples I can think of is from my own life, where my partner is better and more comfortable expressing himself in writing, which can be annoying! So if we have had an argument later on he'll send text messages and I'm like 'oh right that's what you meant'. Text messages enable him to express intimate thoughts more clearly.

JP: Do you think some technologies are part of human intimacy in unexpected ways or perhaps that there are technologies entangled with human intimacies that are not on even our radar when we look at tech and intimacy?

Yeah, I think space and place is relevant here. One of the things that I'm concerned about is small and medium sized businesses in London. They were already having a hard time before COVID, and now they might be forced to close because of the economic crisis being precipitated by the pandemic. Most gay businesses fit into this category. For example, there is a restaurant called Balans which was a cornerstone of the opening up of gay Soho in the 90s in London. It was a destination for gay men and remained a destination restaurant for the past 30 years. It was one of those physical spaces which was absolutely central to gay nightlife in London and its cultures of intimacy. The other week it announced its closure. I don't know how places like that are going to fare after the epidemic. And those technologies of place and space, which made certain

types of intimacy and intimate life possible, are not going to be there, I think, or are going to suffer a further reduction.

And there is an important role that the digital plays in navigating this new terrain. Digital media has played a huge role during the pandemic but, in terms of certain types of intimacy, I don't know if it's the same as bodies in spaces. I don't think digital media always produces a diminished form of authenticity but outside of social distancing the overwhelming tendency has been for digital and physical intimacy to be entangled in different configurations in different cultures. It will be interesting to see how the human desire to be physically connected to other people, in a space with each other, will play out during the remainder of the pandemic. It will be interesting to see what happens in a post-pandemic world and what role technology will play in our intimate lives.

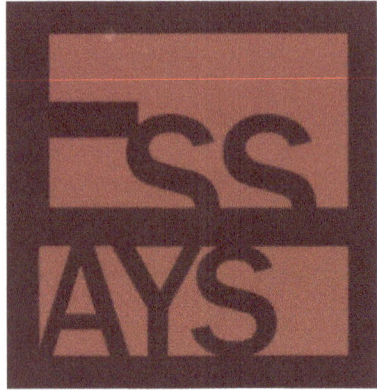

MY QUEER LOVE BOT
JENNIFER POWER

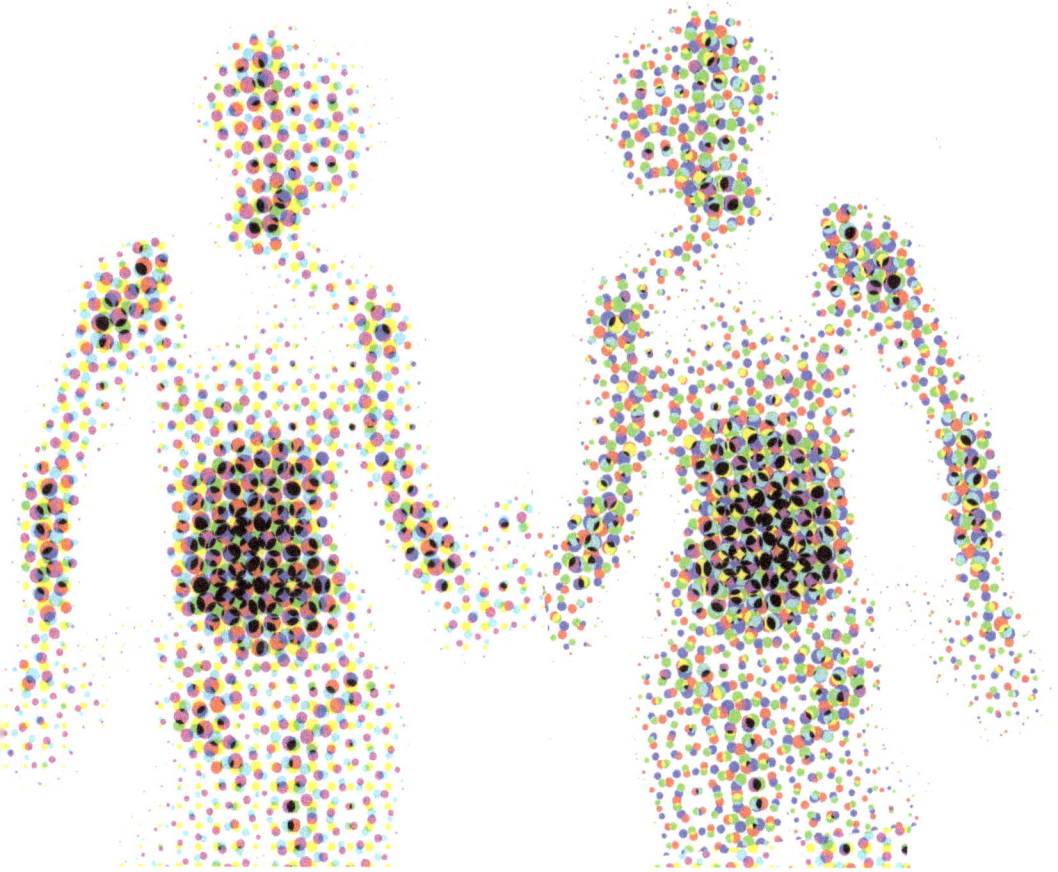

There is a scene in the Marvel film *Guardians of the Galaxy 2* where
Yondu, a space pirate with blue skin, stands at a window and zips his fly
while pitching an anxious stare into the distance. It's snowing outside.
Behind him, several robot courtesans (aka Love Bots *employed* at the
Iron Lotus brothel on the red-light planet Contraxia) wander past. One is
sitting on a bed twirling her hair. She looks sad. Yondu turns to watch
with vague disgust as she manipulates the panel on the side of her head
and switches herself off, seemingly for a post-coital rest.

The Love Bots of Contraxia are styled like femme rockstars, albeit somewhat depressed rockstars with yellowy skin—clearly dressed to entertain the parade of uber-masc space Ravagers who come to Contraxia for 'time out'. The Love Bots are all leather corsets, shiny neck collars, thigh high boots, green lipstick and thick mascara. They each hold the same absent expression.

It strikes me that the Love Bots of Contraxia epitomise contemporary images of sex robots. In recent years the media has regularly baited us with headlines inferring the imminent possibility that human-like androids created for sex and driven by artificial intelligence will soon be commonplace. The UK *Mirror* recently ran with the headline "Lifelike sex robots that 'have a heartbeat' and 'breathe' could go on sale this year" (Best, 2020). Sex robots, sometimes referred to as sex bots, erotic bots or erbots, sit on a bizarrely fine line between science fiction, reality, and voyeurism that is both fascinating and ethically disturbing. Perhaps most disturbing is that common media depictions of sex bots draw on the darkest imagery of sex work—the bots are essentially positioned as sex slaves (or at best, a pimped-up Stepford Wife). Like the Love Bots of Contraxia, the sex bots we are currently being promised are almost always styled to engage the stereotype of cisgender, heterosexual male desire— white skinned Barbie dolls with large breasts and passive, wide-eyed stares. Always available for sex.

Bots in Servitude

Robots, like all machinery, are created to service humanity. In servitude, bots will (or already do) land in places where humans serve other humans—domestic 'help', harsh work in heavy industry, repetitive factory tasks, and in sexual services. When created for sex, bots have potential to be the ultimate sexual partner. They can be programmed to do anything, be anything, and fulfil fantasies that are beyond the capacity or desire of humans. Sex bots might also play a role in love and nurture— providing companionship to otherwise lonely humans or people who can't, or don't want to, seek intimacy in human company.

Sex bots could take any form, but reality bites in gender and cash. In a world where sex is sold for profit, most sex bots, like latex sex dolls before them, are designed in a way that is highly gendered (an interesting queer presupposition in itself given the gender of a bot has no biological

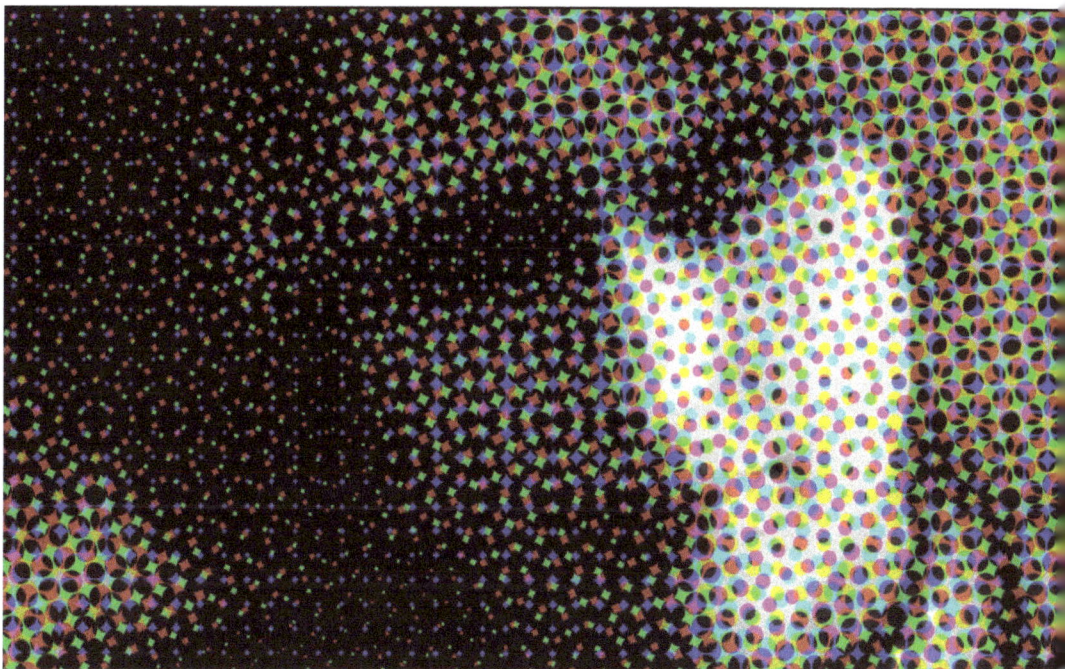

basis) presumably to ensure their marketability. Sex bots have been prescribed with the image that many mainstream commercial sex services tend to favour—passive women, women in service of men, women whose bodies exist only for the pleasures of men and profit. Moral and ethical concerns with the representation of women via sex bots have led to calls for them to be banned. It is feared that such representations will further entrench sexual exploitation of women and fuel sexual violence. Calls for a ban often focus on the murky ethical ground of the representation of sexual assault against women via 'female' sex bots programmed to resist sex and enact rape scenes (Danaher et al, forthcoming, Sparrow 2017).

Misogynist representation of women is undoubtedly a reason to cast a critical lens on the question of what sex bots mean for women, humanity and ethical sex. However, a blanket rejection of sex bots based on the assumption that they can or will only ever be objects that represent the sexual denigration of women, risks falling into a highly sex negative paradigm—a stance aligned with calls for an outright ban on pornography, a position that shuts down any space for feminist or queer porn and disavows women's desire for porn (Kubes, 2019). It also shuts down the possibility that bots could come to represent different forms of gender and sexual expression.

Theoretically, bots could be integrated into creative, democratic, feminist, queer positive and sex positive cultures in the way that other objects designed for sex, such as the dildo, have been. Dildos are arguably a symbol of queer-ness, although this is by no means their origin. Dildos are an ancient technology that, in different forms, has been part of many different cultures across the world. Their use has been prescribed to treat female pain, hysteria, trauma, sexual dissatisfaction and loneliness. Female pleasure is one small part of their history. Dildos are a product of heterosexist culture, reflecting the centrality of the phallus and penis/vagina intercourse in expectations of heterosexual sex. They marginalise other forms of sexual expression and ignore the clitoris as the main locus of pleasure for many women (Das, 2014). However, culturally, dildos are also objects of fetish and perversion. Strap-on dildos are a symbol of resistance to female passivity—objects that *queer* gendered bodies, challenge traditional sexual scripts, and acknowledge penetration as a source of pleasure for heterosexual men (Das 2014). The form of the dildo is both central and immaterial to its cultural status—its basic form has not changed substantially for centuries. But in a weird paradoxical twist in its narrative, appropriation of the dildo into queer culture and queer representation means that it is concurrently a symbol of female oppression and a symbol of queer liberation.

Sex bots of course differ from dildos in that they overtly reflect human form and mannerisms. Potentially (perhaps in the near future) a sex bot will be a machine that looks like us, talks to us, laughs, cries, and responds to our touch. A dildo can be 'queered' by the cultural context in which it is located and the person/s to whom it is attached. Can we say the same for a human-like sex bot? Can a human-like sex bot be 'queered'? If we went to the designers and manufacturers of sex bots with a list of requests for our queer sex bot, what would that be like?

How to Design a Queer Sex Bot

Perhaps a queer sex bot would be a bot, or series of bots, that reflect more diverse representations of humanity. Bots with different body types? Different coloured skin? Different abilities? Different accents? Bots with cool hair? Bots wearing chaps? Or perhaps it would be bots with changeable forms. A bot with modular genitals? (See Figure 1). A bot whose gender appearance shifts across a spectrum of bodily capacities and gendered representations? A bot whose form ranges from human to non-human—goblin, daemon, angel, vampire slayer What would the image of a queer bot even be?

I can see marketing potential in the ultimate queer bot whose body can take any form. A body that presents in its own unique way, with infinite possibilities. The separation of the physical body from identity. The extraction of biology from gender. The ultimate queer body.

But of course, queer is not just about the physical form. Being queer is a stance in the world. It is about the ways we make sense of gender and sexuality. The way we resist, reshape or transgress cultural expectations.

Queerness in a bot would have to exist in its programming—or its deprogramming. Imagine a bot that has no idea about the rules of gender because it has not been programmed with gendered scripts or expectations. What if a bot is never taught to be passive in a feminised way, or has no idea what it means to 'be a man'? Perhaps a queer bot is one that has no idea about heterosexual 'rules' of engagement. This lack of script might make for the ultimate queer bot.

However, a truly queer bot might also need programming to understand where it sits in the world. Queer consciousness is shaped by the experience of being queer in a world where cisgender, heterosexual and able bodies dominate most of the space. This is an experience of belonging and of not belonging, of understanding how to hack normative scripts. Of knowing both the liberation and oppression that comes with this. Of alienation and creative resistance. Of rejection and joy. Do we need to program an experience of marginalisation into our bot for it to be truly queer? Does the bot need to hold some fire of radical resistance to the everyday messages that queer is wrong or bad or deficient? What does this then mean for our bots? Are they just about sex? Or does our queer bot also, by definition, bring a measure of intimacy and emotional connection for a human based on recognition of some shared experience?

Even raising these questions begins to infer the possibility that for our queer bot to be possible it must hold a level of consciousness. This risks taking us deep into the tunnels of artificial intelligence, something I do not wish to do here. However, I do want to talk about agency (in a queer context). Ultimately, a bot is programmed by a human. Capacity for artificial learning aside, a bot has no capacity to make decisions outside of the limited range of options and behaviours written for it by its programmer. In this sense, it is an object of control. It can be manipulated to behave in the ways its human makers tell it to behave. Can a bot be queer if it has no consciousness and no capacity to independently understand its place in the world? Can it be queer if it cannot consciously choose to conform or resist cultural norms? Can it be queer if it has no capacity to seek pleasure on its own terms? Surely this lack of agency is the antithesis of queer experience and queer identity.

Is a Queer Sex Bot Even Possible?

Agency is generally understood as the capacity to consciously make choices and take action. It evokes free will. By definition, a programmed bot has no agency as it has no capacity for free will. We can, of course, argue that no-one makes choices entirely on their own terms. We are all bound by our material existence and cultural location. However, without consciousness our bot has no capacity to understand its actions or to pursue pleasure on its own terms. Without this, how can it be queer?

Perhaps a way forward is to rethink where choice and agency sit in the relationship between humans and machines. Bruno Latour and other writers in the Science and Technology Studies tradition encourage us to imagine humans and machines as collaborators—operating intra-dependently to produce action, reaction, choice, and outcome (Brey, 2005). Latour (2009) uses the gun to explain this concept. He critiques the familiar argument of the US National Rifle Association that 'guns don't kill people, people kill people'. The gun is an object that can have no effect without human action. However, the form of the gun enables the transformation of someone with a *desire* to inflict harm into someone with *capacity* to kill. It does this in a way that another object, such as a knife, cannot achieve on the same scale. The form and function of the gun is central to the way a human engages with it and the way they feel when they hold it. The human and the gun work together. While the gun does not create the human and does not create that human's desire to inflict harm, it could inspire it simply by the knowledge of its existence. Latour writes:

> Which of them, then, the gun or the citizen, is the actor in this situation? … You are a different person with the gun in your hand.

Essence is existence and existence is action. If I define you by what you have (the gun), and by the series of associations that you enter into when you use what you have (when you fire the gun), then you are modified by the gun … (page 189)

Moving from guns to sex, Robin Bauer (2018) draws on a similar concept in their work on les-bi-trans-queer BDSM practitioners, exploring the relationship between transmasculine people and strap-on dildos. Retelling the story of one participant, Bauer writes:

Strapping on a dildo provided his immaterial dick with a material form. He could sense it like a consolidated part of his body, an extension of the boundaries of his body, a transformation of the shape. Scout was not seeking out a substitute for a penis made of flesh and blood; his butch trans masculinity did not create a desire for that. There is no intentionality behind this phenomenon; rather matter displays its queer qualities by stretching out to incorporate other material objects to create unexpected forms of embodiment. (page 72).

Bauer's point is that the strapped-on dildo does not just hold cultural significance as an object or artefact separate from the human body. Rather it becomes integrated with the body so that it is part of an embodied and emotive experience. In this way the dildo is not an 'unnatural object' held up in opposition to the 'natural body' or the 'natural penis'. Rather, it is a unique augmentation of the body that is part of the 'wearer's' sense of themselves—an object that shapes how they experience their body which in turn shapes sexual experiences for both them and their partner/s.

So what of sex bots? Imagine a simple form of programming in which a bot is given capacity to choose between a set of options when faced with a situation or request. Even if the bot's 'choice' is based on random allocation of potential responses rather than consciousness or artificial intelligence, their 'selections' effect the response, actions and options of humans in their sphere. The bot plays a role in producing human experience and action by limiting certain choices and responses and expanding others. The human therefore does not bring all the agency to that interaction. Indeed, the form, function and capacity of the bot influences who the human is in their entanglement with the bot. As Karan Barad (2003) writes:

> Agency is a matter of intra-acting; it is an enactment, not something that someone or something has. Agency cannot be designated as an attribute of 'subjects' or 'objects' (as they do not preexist as such). Agency is not an attribute whatsoever—it is 'doing'/ 'being' in its intra-activity. (page 826-827)

Queerness is similarly produced through our engagement with the social world—through where we stand in relation to others, our response to our location, our response to others, and through our actions and choices. We collectively produce queerness. Throwing radical queer sex bots into that mix, with their wildly malleable and indefinable bodies, might transform our experience of being human and being queer in ways we can't imagine right now. Bots have potential to be more than just objects that symbolise queer culture, but active players in shaping queer culture. In this regard, a queer sex bot—or indeed a Queer Love Bot (which would make Contraxia a vastly more interesting planet to visit)—is a definite possibility.

The Ethics of Queer Bots

A Queer Love Bot might be a naïve or 'Pollyanna-ish' vision for the future of sex bots. However, it is a vision that aims to take us beyond the imagery of the enslaved 'female' sex bot—an image that is disturbingly easier to grasp than that of an empowered, complex queer sex bot. It seems sad to accept that machines designed primarily to facilitate human pleasure and intimacy do not have democratic potential. And radical, sex positive potential. An understanding of bots as more than just passive objects of human desire might facilitate this thinking.

This does not, however, overcome ethical concerns. Manufacturers may never see potential profit in a queer bot. Even if they do, the manufacture of queer bots will not change the misogynist nature of the mainstream sex industry. Sex bots may still take forms that represent violent and morally indefensible sexual and gendered relations. However,

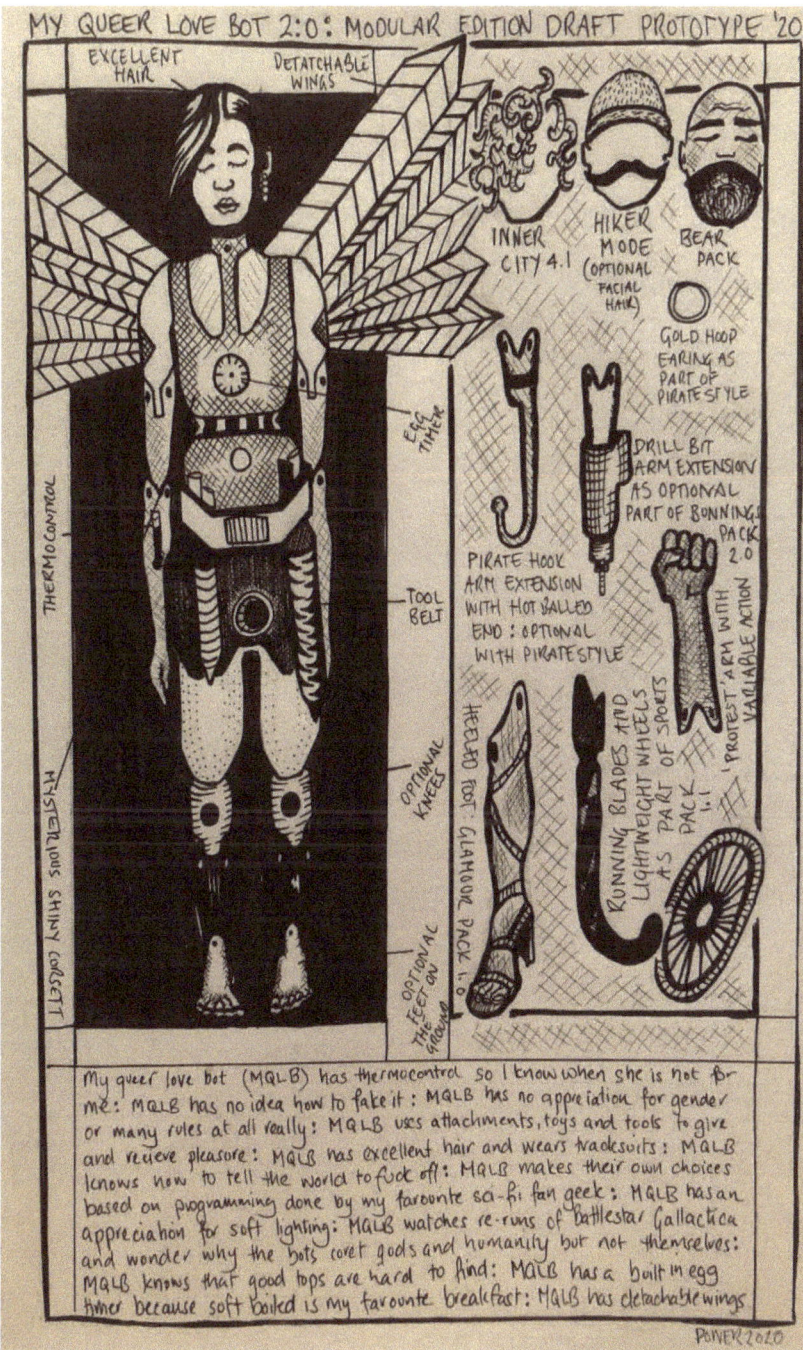

Figure 1. My Queer Love Bot 2.0: Modular Edition Draft Prototype 2020

this may not be the only destiny for sex bots. Bots do have potential to hack existing sexual and gender scripts through entwining subversive programming and non-normative (and changeable) bodily form with human action. Ethical responsibility for the trajectory of human/bot relations sits at all points of their creation and engagement with humans: it lies in the imagining of the social life of sex bots, it sits with manufacturers and salespeople, it develops with programmers and anti-programmers (the hackers and the radical tech outfits), and it continues with the human 'users'. It is a complicated equation that requires a broad vision for the potential life of these technologies, both the frightening and the liberating.

My Queer Sex Bot

What would your queer sex bot be like?

My queer sex bot might come into my world with her de-gendered de-programming and manufactured tendency toward radical dissent. I will appreciate his refusal to conform and she will introduce me to new ideas and experiences while I struggle to explain why humanity makes sense.

Her changeable self will lead me, and my sexual partners, down pathways I never previously considered. In fact, my own programming will be somewhat disrupted by my queer sex bot's bewildered amusement about the things I see as impossible.

References

Bauer, R. (2018). Cybercocks and Holodicks: Renegotiating the Boundaries of Material Embodiment in Les-bi-trans-queer BDSM Practices. *Graduate Journal of Social Science*, *14*(2), 58-82.

Barad, K. (2003). Posthumanist performativity: Toward an understanding of how matter comes to matter. *Signs: Journal of Women in Culture and Society*, 28(3), 801-831.

Best, S (2020). Lifelike sex robots that 'have a heartbeat' and 'breathe' could go on sale this year, *The Mirror,* 11th May, https://www.mirror.co.uk/tech/lifelike-sex-robots-have-heartbeat-22009064

Brey, P. (2005). Artifacts as social agents. Harbers, H (ed) *Inside the politics of technology: Agency and normativity in the co-production of technology and society.* Amsterdam: Amsterdam University Press 61-84.

Danaher, J., Earp, B. D., & Sandberg, A. (forthcoming). Should we campaign against sex robots? In J. Danaher & N. McArthur (Eds.) Robot Sex: Social and Ethical Implications [working title]. Cambridge, MA: MIT Press. Draft available online ahead of print at: https://www.academia.edu/25063138/Should_we_campaign_against_sex_ro bots.

Das, A. (2014). The dildo as a transformative political tool: Feminist and queer perspectives. *Sexuality & Culture*, *18*(3), 688-703.

Kubes, T. (2019). New Materialist Perspectives on Sex Robots. A Feminist Dystopia/Utopia? *Social Sciences*, *8*(8), 224.

Latour, B. (2009). A collective of humans and nonhumans: Following Daedalus's labyrinth, in Kaplan, D (ed) *Readings in the Philosophy of Technology*. Maryland; Rowman & Littlefield.

Sparrow, R. (2017). Robots, rape, and representation. *International Journal of Social Robotics*, *9*(4), 465-477.

Jennifer Power is a Senior Research Fellow at the Australian Research Centre in Sex, Health and Society at La Trobe University. Her research is focused on HIV, sexual and reproductive health and fertility, LGBTI health and wellbeing, and the impact of new technologies on sex and intimacy.

THIS PUBLIC FEELING
MARCUS O'DONNELL

Intimacy and technologies: a pre-history

There have always been technologies of intimacy, they are not the product of our internet age. We think, we learn, we love *with people* but often *through things.* The gift, the love letter, the dowry. The romance novel, the lovers' hideaway, the celebrity crush, the diary, the Grindr profile. Memoirs, rituals, hashtags and funerals. Intimacy is always virtual even when it is at its most sensuously physical. It is mediated by memory, story and hope.

Bernini's St Teresa and a Grindr profile are both snapshots of longing. Both represent bodies turned towards the other. Both tell us something about virtual intimacy.

Intimacy is a liminal space that connects us to something/someone whether that's through screens, through falling in love with history, through bodies rubbing up against each other and dissolving, or through believing that an angelic arrow is piercing your insides with mystic fire. It's also about bodies taking flight, refusing to settle. It's troubling and wonderful.

But that all sounds too exceptional, because intimacy is also quotidian, it's what Kathleen Stewart has called 'ordinary affect':

> a surging, a rubbing, a connection of some kind that has an impact. It's transpersonal or prepersonal—not about one person's feeling literally becoming another's but about bodies literally affecting one another and generating intensities: human bodies, discursive bodies, bodies of thought, bodies of water. (2007:128)

Love, especially queer love, is what some queer theorists have called a *public feeling* (Cvetkovich, A., 2007). The web and other digital technologies both extend and complicate that publicness, but queer love, has never been a private, self-contained emotion. We have always carried into our private moments both the weight and the possibilities of queer history.

We grapple with love and sex and hope and shame and with our first unexpected gifted moments of joy and pain through the only tools we have. There are the things we are told and the things that we come to know, each edging up against the way it *seems* things *are*. Both our personal histories and those public structures of feeling shape that journey to understand and to become intimate. For me this tangle of intimacy has always been about love, sex and religion.

*

I spent the first decade of the twenty-first century thinking about the apocalypse. My PhD grappled with the end times as it presented itself in the Bush era's 'War On Terror'. I traced the ways the last book of the Christian bible, the popularly called *Book of Revelation*, found its echo both in Bush's speeches and in the glamorising of torture in Jack Bauer's *24* and other pieces of popular culture.

Recently I have been asking myself what this all means as we enter the third decade of the century with a new Anti-Christ in office and new contagion spreading different fears.

For all its fantastic imagery of plagues, green and red horses, and multi-headed beasts, the *revelation* at the heart of the Bible's apocalyptic book is a simple one: in the *end* some will be marked with the blood of the Lamb and others with the sign of the Beast, a message that Bush Jr put in even more stark terms: those who aren't with us are against us. In the Trumpian age those others don't even rate a mention, you either understand what's meant by 'Let's Make America Great Again' or you don't. You either wear the baseball cap or you don't.

Whether or not that cap is the sign of the Lamb or the sign of the Beast depends on your perspective. That's the intimacy of tribes.

A shared understanding (or misunderstanding) of the threads of history is what makes intimacy possible with strangers. We are all part of what Benedict Anderson (2006) called 'imagined communities'. The way we imagine ourselves, our similarity and our differences, is what enables communities to exist even across distances as big as nations. As we have seen recently, the fragility of these imagined connections is also what enables nations to suddenly light into fire.

For early Christians, at the end of the first century, who felt increasingly isolated and under attack, the visionary images in *Revelation* connected them back in time to Jesus and forward in time past their current crisis. The book is a letter from John, a teacher in exile on the Greek Island of Patmos, to the scattered communities of his students. He buoys them up in their time of crisis with a vision of an ending which is also a new beginning.

> He will wipe away every tear from their eyes, and death shall be no more, neither shall there be mourning, nor crying, nor pain anymore, for the former things have passed away. (*Revelation* 21:4)

Revelation created the Western template for both utopias and dystopias, whether secular or religious. So, in that sense you might say it was the original 'It Gets Better' campaign.

The It Gets Better (IGB) video project started by gay columnist Dan Savage and his partner Terry Miller was precipitated by a crisis in our community, the increasing visibility of LGBTIQ youth suicide. Savage and Miller's *revelation* for young queers, closeted away in their communities like John of Patmos' early Christians had been, was also in a sense an apocalyptic message: *in the end,* it gets better, believe this and your suffering will ultimately be transformed into joy.

It's not that straightforward though, and IGB has rightly been criticised for presenting a white middle-class version of possibility that ignores the material circumstances of many young queer people*. If you are stuck in poverty or if you are a young black person the road to *better* is a lot more complicated than just hanging on. In this sense IGB, even though it has opened up conversations and brought hope to many, it ultimately shares all the worst aspects of the Bible's magical thinking.

Both the Bible and contemporary social media are not just narrative technologies they are *evangelical* technologies, they are deployed to make a point or to provoke a change of heart through a potent mix of proclamation and seduction. As such they can function as both technologies of intimacy and technologies of exclusion.

Narrative, myth, story are the way public feelings become visible, become tangible, the way they begin to wrap around us. So how do we begin to tell each other stories that are *invitational* rather than *evangelical?* How do we *queer* narrative?

*

For queers both history and intimacy are unstable. This instability opens the crack of possibility, because even in a post same-sex marriage world we are often still making history and making intimacy against the grain. As Lauren Berlant has written: Intimacy builds worlds, she continues:

> it creates spaces and usurps places meant for other kinds of relation. Its potential failure to stabilize closeness always haunts its persistent activity, making the very attachments deemed to buttress 'a life' seem in a state of constant if latent vulnerability. (Berlant 1998: 282)

Margery Kempe, an intriguing fifteenth century English mystic, was acutely aware of the instability and vulnerability of love, she hungered for the pain of love. She just couldn't get enough of Jesus. She was a traveller, businesswoman and mother of fourteen children, who although she probably couldn't read or write, managed to compose what is regarded as the first English-language autobiography. One might say, that when Margery began to dictate her story, autobiography was a new technology and the eclectic meandering book has the vividness and awkwardness of the new. In a time when only male priests were allowed to talk publicly about intimacy with God, Margery was constantly 'usurp(ing) places meant for other kinds of relation'.

Which makes her the perfect subject for Robert Gluck a contemporary American queer writer also interested in narrative technologies. He was one of the founders of the 'new narrative movement'—a loose collection of queer writers who, in the 1980s, began to experiment with a poetic, collage writing style that aimed to do justice to the uncertainties and vulnerabilities of intimate, bodily and sexual life.

> 'We were thinking about autobiography,' he writes in a reflection on the impulses of the early new narrative approach, 'by autobiography we meant daydreams, nightdreams, the act of writing, the relationship to the reader, the meeting of flesh and culture, the self as collaboration, the self as disintegration, the gaps, inconsistences and distortions, the enjambments of power, family, history and language … a new version of autobiography in which 'fact' and 'fiction' inter-penetrate.' (2016:18)

Gluck's *Margery Kempe* is an example of this type of fictional-autobiographical-dream text. In this beautiful, sexy, poetic novel, first released in 1994 and recently re-issued as part of the *New York Review of Books* classics series, Gluck rewrites Margery's autobiography imagining a sexy, young, blond Jesus as her companion and lover. Interspersed with this story is Gluck's own story about Bob and his love affair with 'L.' another sexy young blond. He writes himself as Margery and Margery's story as his. In this way he negotiates and reimagines different kinds of queer longing across time and gender.

Both Margery's Jesus and Bob's L. are unreliable lovers and it is this instability which stokes the engine of desire. In telling love's story both Margery and Gluck/Bob savour the brief moments of connection they are given, re-enacting them and extending them in time. This intimacy is so slippery that they can only take hold of it through the technology of narrative.

Margery's autobiography was a type of coming out, a coming out as fraught with danger and misunderstanding as a queer coming out. Her narrative was one of intimate communication with a personalised Jesus at a time when women's voices were distrusted and discounted, a time when they could more easily be condemned as witches or heretics, than acclaimed as saints. Her courage in recording her story can't be underestimated. But she also counted this as her best possible defence.

As Gluck says of Margery at the beginning of his account: 'She replaced existence with the desire to exist.' She wanted to bring the ethereal story of her mystical desire into some kind of material reality because it had so radically overprinted itself on the routine of her daily life. But it is also a story of failure.

Her story was written down through a complex process of multiple scribes that she cajoled and badgered over a number of years. But one of the ironies of Margery's struggle to bring this book to life is that it was then lost for hundreds of years. A full copy only came to light again as recently as 1934. This is why Gluck calls her a 'failed saint'—her story wasn't really taken up until it was rediscovered, and Margery became an icon for queer and feminist longing.

Gluck's own Margery also took its time to come into existence. He first heard of Margery, and became excited by her work, as a graduate student in the mid 60s but it wasn't until 30 years later that the novel was published. At one point he even tried to write a musical about her. In a recent interview he says it was his experience with 'L.' that enabled him to finally write Margery:

> I could not write about her till I fell insanely in love with a man who was above me—at least I felt he was. Wonderfully handsome, from an old ruling class family, really from a different world. He'd snap his fingers—wow, we're on a mountaintop in Portugal. My passion was as confused and obsessive as Margery's; voila! (Davis 2020)

Gluck wrote from Margery and through her: 'I confected a sentence half-way between Margery's and mine.' (Davis 2020)

But his difference to Margery is always there as well. 'I have less faith in existence than Margery so I describe it more thoroughly,' he writes in the final chapter.

The fifteenth century mystic wrote her desire for the 'manhood of Jesus' his 'precious body,' his 'delightful ears,' she imagined him sweaty and bleeding, she imagined disappearing inside the wound in his side. This is not enough for Gluck. He needs deeper description. But he adds more than description, he gives us a type of mesmeric poetry that is as vividly real as it is abstract. The first time Margery/Gluck imagines Jesus is worth quoting at length:

> *Jesus was sitting next to her. He was birdlike, with a short pointed nose and complete arches over his eyes. He had bone-tipped shoulders and she recognized in his ideal posture and long neck her own 'hidden' aristocracy. Sandy brown hair fell across his lofty forehead but he was a blond. His beauty seemed intentional because she desired it. He wore a short purple tunic. Tiny pink nipples were visible on his milky breast.*
>
> *Jesus gazed up past his brow at Margery. His irises were disorganized blue geodes. He had been crying all weekend—it was Monday morning and he was still crying. He whispered, 'I'm so abandoned.' He raised his head in sadness and his face held the slow joy of deep sky above the sun.*
>
> *He stood and turned on the balls of his feet and began to ascend. Margery fell half asleep when she saw the deity turn away. She felt the strongest sensation of her life, a welling of aspiration and desire*

embodied in the blur of dusty gold, the long smeared shadow of neck and spine, his broad hips, the semicircles of his ass, his long slightly knock-kneed legs. He rotated near the ceiling; she became conscious of the weight of her breasts and the hair down her back. The splayed tips of his long toes floated past her eyes.

Gluck has said that he composes at the level of the sentence, obsessively crafting and recrafting each sentence trying to allow each to sit as its own unit: creating a kind of 'air' between them (Leuzzi 2011). We can see this in the quick shifts in point of view and the moves from depiction to reflection. From Jesus' birdlike features, to his ideal posture and Margery's hidden aristocracy. From her intentional desire to his tiny pink nipples. From Jesus' gaze and whisper to Margery's sleep, waking to her weighted breasts and the splayed tips of Jesus' toes.

Gluck's work is also a confection of Margery in another way. It's a kind of drag performance. 'My book depends on the tension between maintaining an impersonation and breaking it', he writes early in the novel. In a recent interview he elaborated on this:

> I hope you will see Margery in my book, but also see me when I am stepping into her life and body. I struggled with a decision: should I make the book pure and eliminate myself and my hopeless romance? I decided on impurity, so you can witness my projection into the story of this woman which, like any drag performance, includes moments when the illusion is broken.' (Davis 2020)

*

There's a reason that I'm attracted to Gluck and his queering of Margery and to the *Book of Revelation* and its contemporary echoes.

As a teenager on school holidays I used to retreat to a monastery and immerse myself in silence. It was there that I felt most myself. Left alone, not forced to play at being a schoolboy interested in football and girls and cars and whatever else it was that boys at my school, who avoided me, wanted to talk about. At school I was *left* alone, but on retreat I could *be* alone.

Like Margery I replaced existence with the *desire* to exist. Eventually like Gluck I also fell in love with *describing* that desire and finding other silences that fed it. I became a journalist, a writer and an academic as ways of transcribing and examining that desire. Of exploring it and sharing it with others.

If desire and silence were first twinned for me in those teenage visits to monasteries, as I belatedly grew into my sexuality, I looked for that same intensity in other places.

The first time that I had sex was at a sauna in Auckland after arriving in New Zealand to attend a Catholic youth conference. Like the monastery, gay saunas and sex clubs quickly became a place where I went to be alone. Of course, I went there to have sex and to connect but those dark steamy mazes are also unique places of silence that open up space through a communal participation in a hypnotic collective rhythm.

As Gluck notes in one of his essays: 'Bataille [the great French philosopher of excess] showed us how a bath house and a church could fulfil the same function in their respective communities' (2016: 20).

Many years later, after that first sauna encounter, I found that same sense of an extended sexual community online. One night, I found a new lover at a sex club. I went home with him and we stayed together for a few months, but we never stopped playing with other men. In fact, our relationship was played out through these other encounters. Sometimes we would set off to a sauna or sex club together, sometimes we would stay at home and circle through the maze of profiles on Grindr and Bareback.com. Sex for us was an everyday recreational activity but sometimes it edged up against something quite different and brushed against ecstasy. There were usually drugs involved.

The virtual foreplay, the fleshy encounters, the sex club or the pickup site, the relationship, the casual encounters and the not so casual encounters, our regulars, and the excitement of new meets, texts and messages, conversations pre-, post-, and during, knowing smiles and coded asides between my lover and I: each a field of intimacy that bled into each other. All of it was talking, all of it was walking, all of it was silence, all of it was sex.

It took a long time to get to that *wonder*ful abandonment.

When I first began to have sex, after that New Zealand sauna visit, I was wracked with guilt, until months later I unloaded myself again, this time in confession to a priest. In Catholic theology that's a complete reset. After confession you get to start again. And that's what I did over the next twelve months: sex, confession, reset; sex, confession, reset; sex, confession, reset. Those confessions were an extended coming out until: 'I had sex with a man' became 'I'm gay'.

It was the early 1980s and sex had become apocalyptic. With the advent of AIDS, gay liberation tipped from the utopic to the dystopic side of the apocalypse narrative. Crisis was mobilising and Catholicism became for me HIV/AIDS activism. In those early years of coming to terms with the virus, the world-building power of our intimacy as activists was intense: we held our own lives and those of our friends in hand. We crafted new ways of knowing and new ways of speaking sex in public: new ways of building public intimacy between gay men that were life-saving.

We did it all without the internet. Without smart phones. Without apps. We did it with narrative. When doctors, politicians and religious zealots were saying, *sex is deadly*, we said: *Safe Sex*. Two words, not even a sentence, created worlds where intimacy was possible again, in a space that was neither apocalypse nor utopia.

But it remained fraught. For me, coming out in the early 80s, sex was never just an awkward but normal experience. Those experiences were shadowed by physical and spiritual dangers. Maybe that's the way sex is. Perhaps it's never normal for anyone because it's a place where we spill over into someone or something else and we never know from one encounter to the next when that tipping point might happen. That's why it's called *la petite mort* or little death.

Why I like Gluck's *Margery Kempe* so much is that it speaks to my own tangle of love, sex and religion and lights it up with poetry. It traces the virtual web of intimate relations: earthy and physical, as well as virtual and mystical. A type of intimacy that cajoles us into saying things that can't be said.

Gluck and his new narrative colleagues were enamoured by an idea of literary theorist George Lukas that the novel 'holds together incommensurates' (Gluck 2016: 19). Apocalypse also holds together incommensurates: the catastrophic end as holy promise. It twists the traditional narrative of an ending inside out and this trick has been used and misused over centuries to both hold together and to pull apart communities in crisis.

Revelation is a chaotic coded slippery text, a sensuous rich world where raw animalistic desire and the holy urge for transcendence butt up against each other. Like Gluck and colleagues' new narrative it is a dreamlike collage. What it does constantly say is: Look! There! Something else is happening, something behind the veil of the normal. It is so full of such sharp shifts that the essential reader experience is 'What next?' and it keeps us running into the future with its constant refrain of 'and then …'

Our constructed stories bring together things that might not normally be seen together and in some fledgling way begin to make sense of that juxtaposition.

That's why narrative is the ultimate technology of intimacy. *What next* is its challenge, *and then*, is where we accept the invitation to make sense of it together.

References

Anderson, B., 2006. *Imagined communities: Reflections on the origin and spread of nationalism*. Verso books.

Berlant, L., 1998. Intimacy: A special issue. *Critical inquiry*, *24*(2), pp.281-288.

Cvetkovich, A., 2007. Public feelings. *South Atlantic Quarterly*, *106*(3), p.459.

Davis, D., 2020. Read Me: Margery Kempe Is a Raunchy, Beautiful Novel of Sex and Devotion, *them*, https://www.them.us/story/read-me-margery-kemp

Glück, R., 2016. *Communal Nude: Collected Essays*. MIT Press.

Gluck, R., 2020. *Margery Kempe*. NYRB Classics.

Johnson, M., 2014. The It Gets Better Project: A Study in (and of) Whiteness—in LGBT Youth and Media Cultures. In *Queer youth and media cultures* (pp. 278-291). Palgrave Macmillan, London.

Leuzzi T., 2011. Interview with Robert Gluck, *Eoagh* 7, available online: https://eoagh.com/interview-with-robert-gluck/

Phillips, L., 2013. A Multimodal Critical Discourse Analysis of Race, Class, Gender, and Sexual Orientation in the 'It Gets Better Project'. *AoIR Selected Papers of Internet Research*, *3*.

Puar, J.K., 2010, In the wake of It Gets Better, *Guardian*, 16 November http://web.archive.org/web/20160423045457/http://www.theguardian.com/com mentisfree/cifamerica/2010/nov/16/wake-it-gets-better-campaign

Stewart, K., 2007. *Ordinary affects*. Duke University Press.

———————————————

* Jasbir Puar's (2010) *Guardian* commentary from the time points to the problematic nature of the IGB narrative: 'His message translates to: Come out, move to the city, travel to Paris, adopt a kid, pay your taxes, demand representation. But how useful is it to imagine troubled gay youth might master their injury and turn blame and guilt into transgression, triumph, and all-American success?' This is both a class narrative and one constructed through 'whiteness'. One analysis from 2014 (Johnson 2014) showed that 85% of the contributed videos were from Caucasian individuals, even

though there is generally a higher participation of blacks and Hispanics in US social media sites like YouTube. Another analysis even more tellingly noted: 'Participants made gross assumptions about their viewers' racial, class, gender, and sexual identities, overwhelmingly presuming viewers to be Caucasian and of middle-or upper class status and that racial/class differences would have little to no impact on viewers' lives improving' (Phillips 2013).

Marcus O'Donnell is a writer, visual artist and academic. His fiction, journalism and poetry have been published in periodicals and anthologies including, *Verandah*, *Siglo*, *Bent Street*, *New Writing*, *OutRage*, *Hard*, and *The Conversation*. He is currently an Associate Professor and Director, Cloud Learning Futures at Deakin University, in Melbourne Australia.

BOYS
IN
THE
SAND

STARRING CASEY DONOVAN

"A great leap forward...Poole managed to keep the right balance...(it's) as if Ken Russell had made an honest homo flick."—FILMS AND FILMING.

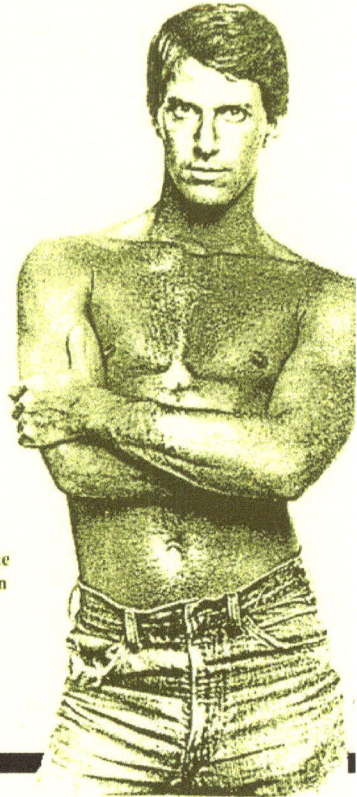

DIGITAL INTIMACY
GARY DOWSETT

An end to the tyranny of distance

It was a long time ago, but I still vividly remember seeing my first pornographic film—and it was film, Super 8 film to be exact. A lesbian friend had taken me to an upper-middle-class, eastern-suburbs Adelaide home for a gay party. Such weekend evening parties in the mid-1970s had a long history connected to the six o'clock closing of pubs (abolished just a few years before) that had been par for the course in moralistic Australia designed to make workingmen having a drink after work go home to their families for dinner at a godly hour.

These gay post-6 o'clock parties were full of men, in the main, of all ages. At this one, a large entertainment space adjacent to a pool had been added to the classy 1930s California bungalow and featured a bar (with cute barman) with a Super 8 projector screening pornography onto a portable screen. Men, and some women, watched while lounging in comfy armchairs, sipping wine. The film featured at length (72 minutes in fact) hunky men fucking in sandhills, no holds barred, in colour, with sound. The film was the iconic *Boys in the Sand* (the title is a homage to the breakthrough off-Broadway gay smash hit, 1968 to 1970, *Boys in the Band*—get it?), filmed in 1971 on Fire Island, the famous holiday island, gay mecca off the coast of New York City. They also screened *Behind the Green Door* (1972) with Marilyn Chambers, the most famous feature-length heterosexual pornographic film of all time, so those gay men clearly had catholic tastes in erotica.

I was stopped in my tracks; it was a profoundly disturbing but strangely intimate moment. I had come across pornography before. At that time, I was a volunteer worker in Australia's first and only gay bookstore, the Dr Duncan Revolution Bookshop, situated in leafy Hyde Park in Adelaide. Most sales came via the bookshop's mail-order service that stretched Australia-wide, so there weren't many walk-in customers. In between packing books and stocking shelves, I read voraciously. I was a young gay liberation activist, so I mainly read the burgeoning gay and lesbian liberation literature, both theory and polemic, related political theory, psychoanalysis, and Left history and politics. I also read my first gay pornography. There wasn't a lot, but it did range from the Rev Boyd Macdonald's publication *Straight to Hell: The Manhattan Review of Unnatural Acts* (1973 to 2017, with various editors), a roneo-ed (who knows nowadays what 'roneo' means?) corner-stapled collection of misspelt, colloquial and personal accounts of illicit sex among working-class, rural and racial minority American men (sex between men was illegal in the USA then), all the way to *Teleny, or The Reversal of the Medal* (1893), an anonymous, eloquent, classically written account of sex among upper-class British men in late 19th century London, attributed to Oscar Wilde. There were also magazines, mostly from the USA, but some British, featuring good-looking, naked or near-naked Physique pin-ups of men, but no stills of sex acts as far as I can remember. That is another reason why the film at that party was so arresting. I even learnt something: I became convinced my knees could bend like that too.

I had never seen other people have sex (late teenage candle-lit groping notwithstanding). I had seen pseudo-sex in mainstream movies and television. Remember, I grew up in the era of Australian TV replays of *I Love Lucy* (1951 to 1957), a series in which the star Lucille Ball and her then real-life husband Desi Arnaz slept in twin beds, courtesy of the US Hayes Code. That was the closest hint of sex I can remember in daily life, unless you count seeing Deborah Kerr and Burt Lancaster in swimsuits getting it on in roiling surf to the surging music in *From Here to Eternity* (1953). The boys in this bit of sand were certainly different. I was not shocked or embarrassed by that porn film; I felt enthralled and, strangely, privileged at being invited into such an intimate moment. That film was not like the performance-driven, narrative-thin, genitally focused, buff-bodied, Viagra-fuelled, mass-produced pornography that seems to dominate the industry today. There was something *engaged* about these boys in the sand (they were actually adult men). They were really having sex—slow, intimate, romantic even, sex with each other, and calmly sharing that generously with others. With me.

Pornography has come a long way since then. After Super 8, think VHS and Betamax, DVDs, the Internet and now live-streaming—all in my lifetime. What was so startling to me in my early 20s is now readily available to anyone, anytime, anywhere and from anywhere, and in such a vast array of versions, iterations, permutations and combinations that one can only conclude that one's own sex life is abysmally lean and unimaginative, no matter how wicked and wilful it might appear to one's grandmother and certain members of the Christian Right. Pornography watching, or 'consumption' as it is bizarrely termed by some commentators today, is beyond widespread; it is commonplace. While men are considered its main audience, women are avid watchers too. It has more 'genres' (another strange term) than the TV series. Yet, gay pornography is incredibly overrepresented as a genre, either indicating there are many more men interested in sex with other men than we might (like to) think, or that the sex that gay men have in pornography might hold interest beyond the confines of same-sex object choice. There is something to this second possibility, as women (heterosexual and otherwise) report enjoying watching gay men have sex in pornography for many and varied reasons, including the 'equality' or 'democracy' of the sex enacted. No one is dominated, apparently forced, or subordinated (BDSM aside). Penetrative sex is not always privileged and either partner (or both in turn) can 'top' or 'bottom'. Such equality and democracy invite intimacy (not intimidation), engagement (not enslavement), inclusion (not individualisation), mutual pleasure (not masculine prerogative), and orgasm for both or many others (not just *his* onanism— the 'money shot'). It's a tasty mix.

I do realise other forms of pornography are abject, dehumanising, unethical, exploitative, hurtful, damaging and dangerous. It is important not to ignore that. However, it is also important to acknowledge that there are many pornographies, and these represent the sometimes-incomprehensible variety of human sexual interest in all its forms, good, bad and emerging. To make sense of pornography, its attraction, its performative effect and its potential requires coming to grips with the possibility that, overall, pornography might be bad because so much of it is so damn good.

*

The ever-advancing technologies that make today's pornography industry one of the world's largest enterprises are not the first technologies to create pornographic images and erotic objects. Classic Greek pottery featured sex scenes of very diverse kinds. Roman statuary glorified the desirable male and female nude body. Houses in Pompeii were decorated with mosaics of erotic action. The Khajuraho friezes in India featured almost every imaginable sexual position. The Khalid Nabi cemetery in

Iran was filled with a forest of large, erect, upright stone penises. The 35,000-year-old Venus of Hohle Fels sculpture is the oldest artistic depiction in a long tradition of honouring vulva. Imaginative erotic pottery was a major art form in pre-Colombian Peru (the collection in the Larco Museum in Lima is mindboggling). Fashion and decorative clothing profiled sexual aspects of the body in various cultures, e.g. 'codpieces' in Renaissance Europe, penis sheaths in Papua New Guinea, the exaggerating corset and bustle in 18th century Europe, the easy-access for sex underwear made especially for Queen Victoria and Prince Albert, the mystery and promise behind the middle-eastern veil. European art museums are awash with nude paintings, sculpture and artefacts from the ancient, classical, medieval, renaissance and baroque periods. Even Michelangelo's Sistine Chapel is plentifully adorned with nudes (mostly male), whose genitals were covered post hoc with wisps of fabric, mostly removed in the recent restoration. There are whole galleries in the Vatican museum lined with statues of nudes (males and females). Most of the males have their penises chiselled off and the confected fig leaves that had once replaced them have been removed, creating a disturbing procession of mass castration. I have often wondered if there is a Vatican basement full of marble penises, awaiting ardent new vocations for the religious in many lifetimes' work in sticking them all back onto the right statues. Clearly, even the celibate (sic) Roman Catholic church recognised the erotic and sexual intentions of art. Indeed, art in Christian Europe was *the* place to explore the sexual; one just had to paint a saint or a figure from a biblical story to get away with it—think Saint Sebastian or Salome.

These art forms are all technologies too. They rely on materials, advances in imagination that translate into materials, objects and processes, and human skill and ingenuity in the manipulation of all of these. It does seem somewhat prosaic and utilitarian to label them all as just technologies. Yet, that seems to be the state of play in rethinking sexuality in the early 21st century. That said, I haven't even mentioned the advent of two technologies that completely transformed representation and literacy (of all kinds) in their time and ever since: the printing press and photography. In fact, it's still print and photography that dominate our media, whether as text or image (still or moving) and on paper or digitally 'published'.

What print offered sexuality was detail, thick description, intricate process, flights of fantasy beyond the real, and the minutiae of emotional and physical responses in/of bodies and by the people who inhabit them. The reader is there, right in the thick of it, often physically taking part— it's not called the 'one-handed read' for nothing. One text stands out here, if controversial and for many years and in many ways censored, the Marquis de Sade's *One Hundred Days of Sodom* (written 1785, published 1904). This is a compendium of almost all sex practices known to human beings at that time (only a few have been added since); it is an encyclopaedia of eroticism. Its history-bound patriarchal narrative can mask the broader anatomy of human sexual desire that de Sade explores. Paulo Pasolini's also oft-banned film version, *Salò* (1975), does not assist in revealing this depth. If anything, Pasolini profiles the abject performance of sex rather than the performative intimacy that de Sade explores in 'practising desire' in its many forms.

This is not the place to detail the relationship between print, literacy and pornography; others have done that better than I could. I will also not attempt a similar analysis of the photographic image (still or moving) and sexuality; that too has been done by far better scholars than I am. What I am interested in exploring is the transformation in intimacy that erotic imagery and text including pornography—the distinction is a much-debated one—has produced.

*

As I noted earlier when I first saw that moving image of sex between those boys in the sand back in the digital dark ages of the 1970s, I felt welcomed into something intimate, a sharing of men practising desire without shame and in public, even though no others were present. Well, that's not right. Those filming were present, but were invisible, and stood in for the rest of us. These bodies-in-sex were without shame for all to see. I had experienced something like that proximity to others' intimacies in reading <u>Teleny</u>, in which I felt all the tense, febrile and arousing moments of the characters as they explored the illicit desires that drove and hounded them in Victorian London. Oscar Wilde's *The Picture of Dorian Gray* (1890) is more indirect and implicit in its homoeroticism than *Teleny*, but not in its representation of desire. *Dorian Gray* is merely tantalising; *Teleny* is downright erotic. What both have in common with *Boys in the Sand* is their inclusion of *us* in the pursuit, in the arousal, in the action, in the pleasure—anticipated, experienced or foregone. What was different about that film, though, was that it was not a representation; it was really happening right before our eyes.

Some might say this is still a poor substitute for the 'real' thing. What's the 'real' here? All that ancient pottery, mosaic, statuary, painting and clothing, while representing sex, arousal, pleasure and satisfaction, are essentially abstractions. What da Vinci's 'La Giaconda' promises is ineffable; that's its attraction. Japanese Shunga Netsuke illustrates sexual athleticism that is ultimately reserved only for Olympians, not us mere mortals. Picasso's erotic images fixate on dominance and disarray; it's discomforting to associate with their pleasures. For all the wonder, there is a kind of distance that this artistic sexuality produces. In its abstraction, sex is placed beyond one's reach. One's own desire seems diminished by it. I've lost count of the number of gay men's houses I have visited that have a small statue of Michelangelo's 'David'. Why? It's beyond me. Is it a claim to alignment, to belonging, to 'tribe'? Sex is ultimately a distant object in this kind of art, as beautiful and entrancing as it might be. Whatever the representation of human sexual desire in it, it is not mine. These sexual objects are to be viewed, desired, owned, displayed, but, ultimately, they belong to an aesthetic to which one can only aspire.

How can it be otherwise? For without objectification, there can be no desire. The very distillation of desire requires the formulation of focus. That is the object. This is not a simple process—just ask Freud. Objectification can settle in the most surprising places: on women as a group in patriarchal heterosexuality; on leather, velvet, silk or rubber etc. in paraphilias (love the term—tells us a lot about sexologists, don't you think?); on difference in skin colour, age, physical attributes, race etc.; on the abject in various forms; on the illicit (when was some sexual action or object not illicit at some time in some place?); on refusal or sublimation. Objectification requires othering in order to beg proximity, closeness, even possession. That is desire.

The written text and photography (still or moving) do something more. These grant proximity, closeness, identification, interpolation. One is invited into minds, bodies, events, settings, affects and pleasures at a strikingly intimate level. Even the distance of time—in the aching need in Shakespeare's *Romeo and Juliet* (1590s) or in the futuristic inter-gender pleasures of Robert Heinlein's *I will Fear No Evil* (1960)—does not push one away. Similarly, photography (still or moving) takes one into its embrace, whether into the ambivalent intimacies of Nan Goldin's *Ballad of Sexual Dependency* (1985-86) or in the ejaculatory exuberance of *Boys in the Sand*. Distance dissolves in these moments and one's interpolation is both voluntary and vocational—it is one's fate to be there.

*

When it comes to the Internet, to digital desire, are we just seeing an extension, an evolution, a new version of these previous technologies? I suspect something else is going on. Yes, we can now see every erotic art object, site and monument at the touch of a screen. Writing as I am in the socially isolated midst of the COVID-19 pandemic, access, immediacy and proximity are blessings. I can view things I might never see for real(?), such as the top of Mount Everest or the inside of a platypus's burrow. Closed theatres, cinemas and arenas don't prohibit me from viewing the online precis of exhibitions in New York City's Museum of Sex or reading the British Library's extensive collection of 'obscene' writing, which has recently gone online. I can watch Bette Davis's wicked desires exercised implicitly in *Jezebel* (1938) or Joe Manganiello's explicit callipygian gyrations in *Magic Mike* (2012). I can also conjure up veteran Jeff Stryker's prodigious gifts in action (44 films from 1986 to 2001) or Asa Akira's current 15 minutes of fame on Pornhub (the world's major online porn gateway, which has reported huge increases in logins during the pandemic 'lockdown'). I can choose from as much free access, subscription or pay-per-view pornography as can be fitted into a day (and a bank balance) in between incessant muffin baking, lounge room aerobics and OCD-level handwashing! As that catchy song from the long-running Broadway hit musical *Avenue Q* (2003 to 2009) tells us: 'The internet is for porn!' All this right in the comfort of my own home. Distanced? Not anymore. Intimate? Too right. Moreover, there are many millions of people around the globe doing just this on computers, laptops, tablets, mobile phones and other 'devices' (should we rename them 'sex toys'?) at any and every minute of the day. Distance no longer exercises its tyranny.

However, there is something else on the internet that is new (relative to the long stretch of history I've been using here) and that is live real-time streaming, often using inexpensive webcams. This can take many forms, but they all involve individuals, couples or groups, of all sexual orientations and preferences, engaging in 'sex practices' (don't you just love the social sciences' distancing invoked in that term?), right now in 'real' time, as watchers live and breathe in tandem, from as far away as their devices' screens in full colour and with interactive sound. The watchers can have their webcams reciprocating the action too. These interactions can be private just like a phone call between two people or involve many others like a party line. What becomes distance here? Add the multiplying affordances of teledildonics and the intimacy even reaches through the screen. Pleasures can be enjoyed and shared at a level of detail that would shock Robert Mapplethorpe. This is the ultimate 69! Everyone gets a money shot—and that phrase no longer applies just to men.

Are these webcam 'models' (as the porn industry calls them) merely objects to desire? Well, yes and no. Certainly, these people can be watched and desired and 'used' for personal pleasure. Yet, that is often their pleasure (and profit) too. Are they exploited? Some, undoubtedly yes—there are big pornography enterprises behind these apps. Others, no. The apps also facilitate a personally motivated adventure, whether it's a dating or hook-up site such as Tinder or Grindr, or an amateur pornography streaming service such as LiveJasmine or Cam4. For some, such live online sexual performances are sought as a moment of both objectification and subjectification. Such pleasure is productive. The desired object is also the desiring subject. The technology performatively subjectifies as it objectifies, i.e. it creates new subjects of sexuality through the enactment of the self as an object. For without subjectification there can be no pleasure. These emerging sexual subjects, like those boys in the sand, are also without shame. Their bodies bear no stigmata. There is a refusal to be subjected to the privatisation of sex; these are not hidden guilty anxious pursuits (although they still might not alert their relatives). There is a pride and pleasure in these performances.

For some observers, this might constitute a shocking moment of self-delusion in which the performing subjects are manipulated and lose control of their images and identities as digital objects. There are one or two US congressmen who found that out to their detriment, but theirs were anachronistic and clandestine abject acts. These amateur pornographers can now develop careers from their streaming not just in making porn but as influencers, fashionistas, celebrities and gurus in the gig economy. The 'hottest' porn stars now have their own Instagram accounts and sponsored YouTube channels. The NYC Museum of Sex even featured an exhibition on *Cam Life: An Introduction to Webcam Culture* (2020) as COVID-19 struck. Exhibit? Culture? Art? Electing a politician who has not sent a 'sext' at some time might even become impossible in a few years. It may even become a mark of political esteem—I cum therefore I can! 'Thou shalt not …' holds sway no longer. Sexuality has finally become the truth of the self if not quite in the way Michel Foucault originally argued.

This is a signal shift in the history of sexuality. It's not just that technology has brought sex closer, even bringing sex at a distance closer, startlingly close in the case of pornography. Sex with a stranger (or, many of them) has become differently possible in ways barely captured in that sex researchers' term 'casual sex'. We are welcomed into the bodies and lives of others in ways hitherto impossible and can return the privilege. They are hardly distant strangers anymore; they are one's intimate familiars. In this cacophony of concupiscence, these technologies speed up the performative in sex, disturbing once iron-clad discursive boundaries, dismantling prohibition, hindering inhibition, offering enticements, expanding possibilities, and engendering pleasures through as many often-unforeseen means as possible. The categories of old, let alone the recent past, are revealed as the discursive nonsense they always were, made-up, contingent, whether gay, straight, bisexual, polysexual, asexual, male, female, intersex, trans*, non-binary, gender-neutral and all the rest of the alphabet soup of contemporary identity politics. These multiplying labels continue to fail. They are revealed as feeble stratagems—the last cry of 'me', 'myself', 'I' in the current mass culture of neoliberal individualism—that ultimately reflect a powerlessness that will be increasingly obviated by the insurgency of sexuality and its performative renovation of subjectivity. This subjectivity is one in which the embodied desiring self can only be experienced and exercised simultaneously as a desired object in an ever-expanding economy of pleasure. Who needs me when there is we? In the techno-sexual race for our future, the horse has bolted and there is no stopping it now. After all, even our queen, Elizabeth II, at age 94, recently showed us that we can all, post-COVID-19, ride astride a horse.

Gary W. Dowsett, PhD, FASSA, is Emeritus Professor at the Australian Research Centre in Sex, Health and Society, La Trobe University, Melbourne, and Adjunct Professor at the Centre for Social Research in Health, UNSW Australia, Sydney.

INTIMACY IN ONLINE SPACES FOR BI+ PEOPLE
EMIEL MALIEPAARD

Introduction

As a member of various (inter)national online groups for plurisexual people (or bi+ people) and as an academic I know the value of online spaces for bisexual people (Maliepaard, 2017). These online spaces can be important spaces for plurisexual people to discover their sexuality, discuss issues related to their sexuality, but also to find social support and new (social) connections. As such, I daily see posts about bisexual activism, bi erasure (in media, research, or elsewhere), but also threads about struggles people encounter and posts with typical questions such as 'when did you discover you are bi+?' or 'in what type of relationship are you?', in essence the typical questions to get to know each other and foster interaction between members. Unsurprisingly, several studies concluded that online spaces can be safe spaces for sexual minority people: safe in the sense of support and acceptance (Atkinson & DePalma, 2008; Munt, Bassett, & O'Riordan, 2002). Safe in the sense of the *relative*—but not absolute—absence of heteronormative and mononormative assumptions and the increased likelihood of being oneself. Whereas heteronormativity refers to particular forms of heterosexuality as the norm, mononormativity refers to the conviction/norm that one's sexual identity/orientation is based on the sex/gender of one's partner, is binary (one is either heterosexual or gay/lesbian), and immutable.

However, members do not only participate in online spaces for plurisexual people to look for help, social support, or acceptance. Sexuality and intimacy have different positions and roles in digital spaces and people may use different online platforms for dating and sex as well (see Nash & Gorman-Murray, 2019 for an anthology that discusses these different positions and roles of sexuality in digital spaces). Quite often, I see posts by (new) members such as 'looking for a male/female partner' or people (singles or couples) mentioning their wish to find people for sexual endeavours as reason for joining Facebook groups for plurisexual people.

These posts are often met with some scepticism, disapproval, or frustration in these Facebook groups. What position do explicit dating posts and intimacy have in online bisexual groups?

This Contribution

Attitudes towards dating posts

In one of the Facebook groups of bisexual people (ca. 650 members) I joined—a group that stated in their rules that explicit dating posts are not allowed—I posted a question related to how members experience explicit dating posts in this group and received replies/elaborations from over 30 members. I asked for permission to use these replies and also translated these quotes from Dutch into English. Several themes can be distinguished in the replies.

First, many people mainly felt frustrated that people posted dating requests because they did not read the group rules which do not allow for explicit dating posts. It happens quite frequently that (new) members post their search for a romantic and/or sex partner(s) sometimes with seductive pictures Nevertheless, most of the members did not feel frustrated because of the actual content of these posts: they just ignored these posts and scrolled down to read other posts. As one member wrote:

> So, I am just scrolling to the next post or write a reply like 'hey this ain't the place for it'. It is mainly frustrating like 'Sigh, again someone who think that we bisexual people are only in a group to look for sex.' (I don't feel unsafe, not at all, but I can imagine that people who are just new and want to talk about their experiences may not want to see this.

Secondly, and related, several people felt that explicit dating posts were not in line with the 'nature' of this group: a social group that was mainly dedicated to sharing information and experiences of living a life as a bisexual person. A few of the members also argued that people looking for social contacts were 'okay', for instance, to give members the possibility to meet likeminded people and also to find empowerment. While some members agreed that sexuality and intimacy is part of one's everyday life (also as a plurisexual person), such dating posts were seen as disrupting the social functions of this group, in particular explicit dating posts. These people who were not against dating posts itself and suggested that different groups are needed, or more suitable, for such posts. As one member wrote:

> I think there are some limits. This group is, in my opinion, not for dating or sex but for exchanging information, education, starting of meetups, workshops, and such activities, in order for bi+ people to meet likewise people in whatever way. Regarding the other thing [sex and dating] there are different groups on and beyond Facebook. That is, for me, the limit.

Thirdly, a few members mentioned that bisexual people already facing stereotypes of being hypersexual, wanting to engage in threesomes, and needing both men and women to have a satisfactory sexual and romantic life. One of them also mentioned that such explicit emphasis on sex does not fit her own definition of bisexuality that is much more than sex: it encompasses attraction and love. Another one mentioned that dating posts are much about physical appearance and not about content or one's personality, and this group should be about content. Regarding stereotyping someone replied:

> I notice that I think that these kind of messages [explicit dating posts] contribute to bisexual stereotyping, the stereotypes that I need to challenge (such as: if you're in a relationship with one sex/gender you still desire someone from a different sex/gender, and we bisexuals are very much into having sex).

Fourthly, several participants—in particular women—mentioned that they felt unsafe because of explicit dating posts. They mentioned unwanted friend requests, unwanted explicit direct messages from others, and sexual innuendo in normal conversations. As one of the moderators replied, this creates an unsafe and hostile environment, in particular for bi women. The concept of unicorn hunters is mentioned: couples who are looking for a bisexual woman to engage in sexual activities with them. It also impacts the overall impression of the group:

So, I am thinking just now: I don't feel very safe here to be honest. Anonymous profiles, vague pictures, or just pictures of someone's body. No further info or introduction. Very unpleasant. A vague version of a dating website and that's not what this group should be.

Feelings of being sexualised and being part of an unsafe group results in people becoming less active in this group. Different members replied, for example, that they are less eager to read new posts in this group, or even to stop interacting with other posts; they become more of a 'lurker' instead of an active contributor in order to be less visible and approachable for people with different intentions. As one person explains:

I notice that I become less active here in the group, it does not feel like home anymore in this group. I now and then just 'like' some posts. Also, I don't welcome people anymore. I first want to see what someone brings and whether that person did not just join the group to get laid.

Fifth, only a very small minority of people replied positively to the explicit dating posts. One of them argued that the bi+ group is a highly heterogenous group and we should cherish that. Another one also understood why people were looking for a partner for a sex date and think it is reasonable to do so, however questioned whether this group would be the right place. Finally, a member argued that she is a bi-*sexual* and that sexuality is or can be an important aspect of bisexual lives. She rejected the 'fake prudery' of members and explained how previously such online groups helped her to shape her bisexual life since she discovered her bisexual desire/orientation. In her words:

What's the point of meeting likewise people if you cannot be the person you are? Of course it is not good to post less flattering pictures, but everyone needs to know it for themselves. (…) I try to accept everyone, but they do not accept me so I tell them that they should not approach me. You cannot educate everyone, let alone change them. I am not a moralist or hypocritical.

Discussion

It seems that sexual intimacy has no place in this bisexual support group due to the explicit rules and the practical understanding (the know-how on how to act in this group) of this Facebook group as a social group and tacit knowledge how people should use and experience this group: the group is designed and (re)produced as a safe space for people who are looking for discussions, helping each other, and for sharing information on bisexuality, the everyday life of bisexual people, and 'bisexual news'. Intimacy as in explicit dating posts may disrupt the understanding and use of this group as a social group and create an unsafe or *unheimlich* (creepy) atmosphere for visitors who align with the explicit rules and practical understanding of this group. While a large number of members just feel frustrated and scroll down, for others it may be the reason to become less active. The explicit dating posts are also a proxy for unwanted attention such as friend requests, sexually explicit messages, and sexual innuendo in 'normal posts'.

Less than a handful of members took a positive stance towards explicit dating messages, however it is possible that people with a more positive view were either not interested to engage in this discussion because they participate in this group for different reasons such as dating. They may also be reluctant to reply due to the many replies that established and/or reproduced the norm that explicit dating posts are unwanted. In fact, I believe that most of the responses to my question and to (new) members who post explicit dating posts (re)produce particular norms and values of what is acceptable (behaviour) and what not. As Hanckel (2019) and Maliepaard (2017) noted in relation to respectively a social media platform and an online forum, these spaces are subject to power dynamics and relations and actively governed by their members.

The finding that explicit dating posts do not belong in this group is remarkable in the light of the Dutch bisexual movement. The largest bisexual forum for bisexual people had a separate *adult section* comprising posts on sex toys, erotic stories, fantasies, pictures of people's genitals, and more erotic threads, and many topics of this forum were related to sex, sexual preferences, gender preferences, relationship diversity, and more. The website of the dissolved Dutch Bisexual Network had a separate section on contact advertisements (for sex and dating), which also was the most popular section of their website according to the webmaster of this website. A study on the Dutch bisexual movement since the early 1990s (Maliepaard, in press) revealed that, similar to the bisexual movement in the United Kingdom (Monro, 2015), there was more overlap between bisexual and kink, swingers, polyamory, and BDSM communities instead of with gay and lesbian communities. Activists in the Dutch bisexual movement were very eager to make space for sex and sexuality within bisexual groups, communities, communication, and activities in order to be inclusive to all types of bisexual people. This approach, however, sometimes also resulted in tensions between people who did not align with the sex positive approach of Dutch bisexual activists.

I am convinced that online spaces—often theoretically and empirically understood as more anonymous and liberating as compared to material/offline spaces (e.g. Kitchin, 1998; Maliepaard & Van Lisdonk, 2019)—offer many possibilities for plurisexual people to look for romantic and/or sexual partners. As George (2001) argued, the Internet offers many possibilities for recreational sex, and many of these recreational sex seekers are behaviourally bisexual. The absence of specific material venues or events for plurisexual people may urge them to look for (sexual) intimacy in online spaces: bisexual groups are an accessible option as well as more specific forums or (dating) websites, some of which are specifically targeted at bisexual people.

It would be wrong to ignore sexuality and intimacy within these groups as online spaces are not independent from material/offline spaces and the manifold desires people may experience and embrace. According to George (2001), it would be empty moralism to condemn recreational sex posts and dating posts and, to extrapolate this argument, be scared of the stereotype that bisexual people are hypersexual or promiscuous. Indeed, some plurisexual people are hypersexual, are promiscuous, however others are simply looking for a relationship partner or for an occasional or more sustainable sex partner. While men may be more active in posting messages and replying to other messages, there are plenty of (mixed-sex) couples and (single) women who also post explicit dating posts (George, 2001). Ignoring the diversity in plurisexual people would mean that one specific form of bisexuality and of bisexual lives would be privileged over others (e.g. Gurevich et al., 2011).

I agree with George (2001) on her empty moralism argument, but also agree with George when she argues that it is important to focus on negative side effects such as exploitation and, I would add, sexual aggression and feelings of unsafety. It is important to address these issues, in particular because people experience and participate in online spaces in different ways. Despite the fact that this particular group for plurisexual people is a private group, Facebook (as social media platform) may feel less anonymous—as most people use their real first name and surname—as compared to online forums or chatrooms on which people often use avatars and nicknames.

Final Thoughts

Before heading into the final thoughts it is important to reiterate that this essay is based on replies to one question in one plurisexual support group in the Netherlands. Although over 30 members replied (about 5% of all members), and various members also replied to answers by other members and therefore created modest discussions among themselves, I believe there is much more research needed to provide more in-depth insights into the tensions between online bisexual groups and the various positions that intimacy may have. One can think about a content analysis of online bisexual groups or a mix of interviews and focus group discussions with group members.

It is clear that explicit dating posts may contribute to feelings of unsafety and unwanted attention, as such it would be important to think about alternatives to facilitate plurisexual people who are seeking a relationship and sex partner in online bi+ groups. A separate section on dating—similar to the website of the Dutch Bisexual Network and the forum for bisexual people—and clear rules about approaching fellow members and sexuality related content/messages could be an alternative option for creating a safe atmosphere that does not interfere with the social function of this particular social group for plurisexual people and at the same time make space for people who are looking for intimacy in various ways. Interestingly, one of the members of this Facebook group made a separate private group for bisexual dating and thereby provides opportunities for digital intimacies for plurisexual people separate from the social group. Perhaps, for this specific plurisexual social group, a bit of promotion of this separate group on bi dating may already help to find a balance between different interests of group members.

References

Atkinson, E., & DePalma, R. (2008), Dangerous spaces: Constructing and contesting sexual identities in an online discussion forum. *Gender and Education, 20*(2), 183–194. doi: 10.1080/09540250701797192

George, S. (2001), Making sense of bisexual personal ads. *Journal of Bisexuality, 1*(4), 33–57. doi: doi.org/10.1300/J159v01n04_04

Gurevich, M., Bower, J., Mathieson, C.M., & Dhayanandhan, B. (2007). 'What do they look like and are they among us?': Bisexuality, (dis)closure and (un)viability. In V. Clarke, & E. Peel (Eds.), Out in psychology: Lesbian, gay, bisexual, trans, and queer perspectives (pp. 217–242). Chichester, England: Wiley.

Hanckel, B. (2019). "I want my story to be heard…": Examining the production of digital stories by queer youth in East and South-East Asia. In C.J. Nash & A. Gorman-Murray (Eds.), The geographies of digital sexuality (pp. 203-224). E-book: Palgrave Macmillan. doi: 10.1007/978-981-13-6876-9

Kitchin, R. (1998), Towards geographies of cyberspace. Progress in Human Geography 22(3), 385–406. doi: 10.1191/030913298668331585

Maliepaard, E. (2017). Bisexual safe spaces on the internet: Analysis of an online forum for bisexuals. *Tijdschrift voor Economische en Sociale Geografie, 108*(3), 318-330. doi: 10.1111/tesg.12248

Maliepaard, E. (in press). The bisexual movement in the Netherlands: Developments and experiences of key bi activists since the 1990s. In E. Maliepaard & R. Baumgartner (Eds.), Bisexuality in Europe: Sexual citizenship, romantic relationships, and bi+ identities. Routledge.

Maliepaard, E., & van Lisdonk, J. (2019). Online dating practice as a perfect example of interwoven worlds? Analysis of communication in digital and physical encounters. In C.J. Nash & A. Gorman-Murray (Eds.), The geographies of digital sexuality (pp. 137-158). E-book: Palgrave Macmillan. doi: 10.1007/978-981-13-6876-9

Monro, S. (2015). *Bisexuality: Identities, politics, and theories.* Basingstoke, England: Palgrave Macmillan. doi: 10.1057/9781137007315

Munt, S.R., Bassett, E.H, & O'Riordan, K. (2002). Virtually belonging: Risk, connectivity, and coming out online. International Journal of Sexuality and Gender Studies 7(2-3), 125–137. doi: 10.1023/A:1015893016167

Nash, C.J. & Gorman-Murray, A. (2019). The geographies of digital sexuality. E-book: Palgrave Macmillan. doi: 10.1007/978-981-13-6876-9

Dr Emiel Maliepaard is an academic researcher at Atria: Institute on Gender Equality, The Netherlands. He published widely on the everyday lives of bisexual/plurisexual people and on the interwovenness of online and offline spaces. He co-edited (with Dr Renate Baumgartner) the forthcoming book: *Bisexuality in Europe: Sexual citizenship, romantic relationship, and bi+ identities* (Routledge).

OUT IN THE OUTER WORLDS
NESSIE SMITH

A new online game featuring perhaps the very first openly asexual characters.

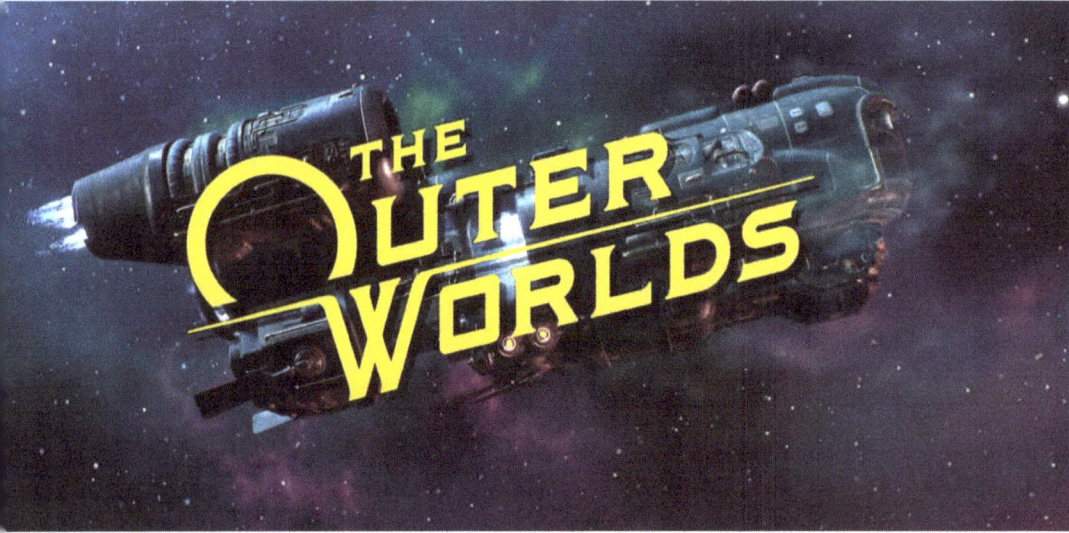

The Outer Worlds is a massive open world single-player space exploration role-playing game released in a staggered manner around the start of 2020. It is being played with gusto by asexual queer gamers as COVID-19 restrictions offer us an unprecedented level of excuse for indoor play—including me. Lost in transit while on a colonist ship bound for the furthest edge of the galaxy, our character in the game (you) wake up decades later only to find yourself in the midst of one of many deep conspiracies threatening to destroy the Halcyon Holdings Corporation colonies. As you encounter various factions led by potential allies or enemies with attractive asymmetrical and butch pirate haircuts in the furthest reaches of space, your character increasingly becomes the unplanned variable in this initially corporation-dominated intergalactic game of thrones. How impossible, and how important, are digital intimacies in this game?

You: Playing Ace

The Outer Worlds is being lauded across online gaymer mags, Reddit Boards, fanzines and Insta as one of the first ever 'big' games—*perhaps the very first*—to star *openly asexual characters*. Talk of asexuality in popular culture often explores conservative ideas on 'virginal' or 'motherly' women, depicted as not sexual, or as not sexually active—whatever their attractions are (Jovanokski, 2017). Asexual identity or a description of desire levels, however, challenges any assumption that all people have feelings of sexual attraction. It is related to those feeling little to no sexual attraction to others or interest in sexual acts; approx 1+% of people (Emens, 2014) … though statistics can be conservative for atypical sexuality constructs. Asexuality can broadly include people who to some degree feel romantic or aromantic (Deluzio Chasin, 2011). It can include a portion of those who have diverse gender identities, sex characteristics, or romantic orientations (Hillier et al., 2010; Jones et al., 2016). Engagement in actual sexual activity levels should be seen as a separate issue from actual desire due to the complex politics of relationships and many other themes (Emens, 2014).

Surprisingly what most online discussion overlooks is that the openly asexual characters in the game include not just one of your companions (more on her later). These include *first and foremost the player-run protagonist: you* … If you choose to accept the specific dialogue options to run your character's script in an ace (asexual) way. There's not much in popular culture in terms of asexual representation, let's be honest. Perhaps

Jughead Jones in the *Archie* comics and *Star Trek"s* Spock (Wrhel, 2017)? However there has been certainly no protagonist of note pro-actively declaring Ace-hood that we as audience or player can steer and 'be' in an intimate first-person digital experience in mainstream media of any kind. If you play a female-bodied character you can also take on the male identity of the former commander of your ship *The Unreliable* 'Alex Hawthorne' and flirt with his computer and fuck with his gender after realising you have probably landed your escape pod on his bod accidentally killing him in some early scenes ... and a variety of other surprisingly fun and gender or sexuality queering options. I'm not sure if these are 'canon' (developer-intended), but there's something about this game that suggests it doesn't matter.

There are character customisation options so you can choose your gender, your level of gender diversity (facial hair options and a range of hairstyles available to all), skin tone and features, skills and attitudes. Though some characters call you 'The Stranger' or 'Captain' initially, I can't give you the name of your ace character to celebrate. That's also something you get to decide; to a degree. Interestingly, across 2020 fans of the game have discovered through trial and error that *The Outer Worlds* censors over 500 words as names for your protagonist. These include words which could perhaps be considered politically loaded such as 'gay', 'transgender', 'Muslim' or even just arguably offensive or inoffensive terms related to nationalities. The list is especially notable for its inconsistencies on LGBTIQ+ and other identity-related terms. For example the list includes the banning of the Polish and German terms, and yet not the English term, for 'lesbian'. This feels like an undeniably strange decision. Fans' debates on discussion-boards centre on whether this inconsistency is due to the developers of the game, Obsidian, simply importing a name ban list from some generic company that maintains such terms according to country-specific regulations so the game can have a global playership? Or whether it is based on more direct context-specific efforts at making a 'woke' game even more woke through provincialised prevention of discriminatory slang. My guess is they probably were forced to comply with country-specific rules to get the coveted generically accessible ratings most companies crave for expanding playership and profits.

Digital Intimacy Rating: Up to 10/10.

Parvati Holcomb: Asexual Lesbian Mechanic

The Outer Worlds also features the *first openly asexual lesbian companion*—Parvati, an empathetic yet initially rather naïve mechanic. She suffers from endearing if over-the-top confidence issues. You'll find Parvarti working in Edgewater on Terra-2, the first planet you get to truly explore. She is maintaining the Saltuna Cannery's machinery, giving them names and seeing them as friends she cares for. It's important to note that Parvati is positioned as the first companion option, in a game of many companion potentials. The first time you head up to speak with Reed Tobson as part of the main quest, Parvati is in a debate with Tobson about fixing machinery before your arrival interrupts them. Listen to what Tobson has to say … Parvati will then be the first potential companion to offer to accompany you. At this point in the game you can accept or decline her offer. This 'first companion' position is a privileged position in a massive open world game. It is most likely you will accept her above any others. To begin with, roaming Space alone is relatively boring compared to shooting up monsters with an artificial pal! Also, more people play the first portions of games than the latter portions. In addition, the option to find and really connect with Parvati is almost inevitable (save for in the 12 minute speed runs some gamers have proved doable, though this game could otherwise take months of playing for hours). Later locations and pals are far less likely to be encountered by such a strong majority of *Outer Worlds* players. So they don't necessarily share the depth of character development and digital intimacy possible with Parvati.

There is also the greatest potential for you to spend much time in *Outer Worlds* with Parvati building up her strengths and qualities. Adding Parvati to your party adds a variety of potential skills to your team (Persuade, Lockpick, Engineering etc.). Parvati can also bring helpful fighting moves useful in the far reaches of space like slamming down her mechanically-enhanced hammer, creating a blast wave that shocks corporeal enemies and stuns auto-mechanicals (*Outer World's* term for robots). You could choose to leave her as is … a fairly shy and dependent character who rarely speaks up when reprimanded and doesn't make decisions by herself to. Or potentially, with your help—let her bloom into a go-getter declaring her feelings and preferences. Over the game if you spend enough time with Parvati you will learn that although she has had past romantic relationships, none of them lasted long. This, she explains, was due to her disinterest in the physical side of relationships. This resulted in lovers misinterpreting her as 'cold'. Here you can choose to relate with or encourage her in her experiences and feelings. Therefore it is also most likely you'll feel the greatest attachment to Parvati overall in the game, merely by spending so much time shooting the breeze with and reassuring this likeable and often goofy space peer (or understandably disgruntled employee; depending on your choices and treatment of her). There is potential for great intimacy with this character through the conversations you have and the sense of companionship built over what can either be a very short or very long game … you choose.

Digital Intimacy Rating: Up to 10/10.

Junlei Tennyson: Groundbreaker

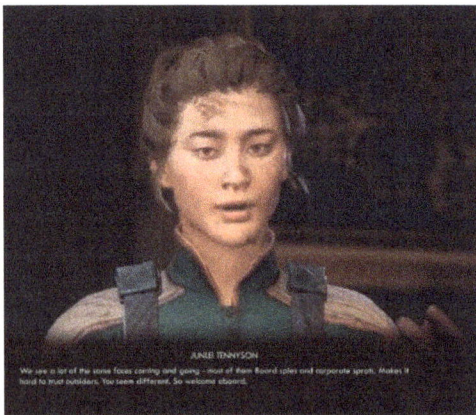

After leaving Edgewater with the Captain and travelling to colony ship Groundbreaker, Parvati meets and develops feelings for the leader of the Groundbreaker outpost and Chief Engineer, Junlei Tennyson. Junlei is the third generation of Tennyson leadership aboard the Groundbreaker. She is an out gay character. She has an 'active' dating history. Junlei is interesting for her resilience. Also for her impressive career achievements in rising from Engineer to Captainship. Moreover, for her dedication in running the only community in Halcyon

operating outside The Board's control. Junlei has an excellent knowledge of ships, so Parvati is both impressed and intimidated by her knowledge and kind, calm, confident ways. Junlei sends you, the protagonist, on some quests involving obtaining parts for repairs for the heating system on her ship (starting in the quest 'Happiness is a Warm Ship').

Through the Parvati-Junlei dating drama storylines (including quests titled 'Drinking Sapphire Wine' and 'Don't Bite the Sun') you can choose to also come out as asexual/Ace. This is done sensitively not only in support of Parvati, but in your efforts to help her pursue her idol Junlei. You can help Parvati achieve a closeness with Junlei by giving advice and aid on practical aspects of their messaging and dating needs, or leave that alone. If you pursue it, warning: you'll be putting in some hours on a large range of collection quests for items now rare across the corporate colonies (some pre-date soap here, some fancier clothing there, some delicious date-worthy 'Dustback Casserole' and so forth). There is also a session of poetry analysis. At some stage, some heavy first-time drinking is involved. Then there are all the pep talks and various heart-to-hearts between characters where we rake over the coals of what happened with exes named Isabelle and what-not. Some fear in the night, some happy-screams into pillows. There seem to be a few other characters competing with Junlei for Parvati's attentions, too. These include the pink-haired haberdashery owner Celeste Jolicoeur from Byzantium's Prosperity Blaze. Also, the incompetent engineer Thomas Kemp from the Terra-2 Botanical Labs. However Junlei is Parvati's sole focus. Indeed, players warn that if you kill Junlei whether on purpose or by accident (some of your weapons can be unwieldy), there are dire consequences for your relationship with Parvati.

Digital Intimacy Rating: 5/10.

Ellie: The Butch Space Pirate

There are throughout the game a range of other queer-feeling couplings and gender non-normative characters, perhaps because this game is set in a future time period. In this future, generic social ties as we know them seem to be organised very differently in ways that challenge traditional familism. Refreshingly, Western society's current gender norms are no longer really that dominant and definitely not reflected in fashion for women in particular. Some interesting characters include for example the enjoyable criminals Nelson Mayson the sartorially inspiring drug dealer, and Catherine Malin the tough rebel leader in Fallbrook Monarch. These two may sound like problematic constructions sure, but they are hardly as problematic as the many queer feeling corporate stooges and police characters … or their straighter counterparts. Nobody in space has a straightforward ethical compass. Their 'goodness' is often a matter of your own perspectives and values.

But perhaps most notably there is Ellie the butch space pirate. You meet Ellie inside the Groundbreaker, where you find the medical bay (Medbay). Ellie is arguing with one Dr. Mfuru about a patient, Jessie, and how Ellie wants to be able to see her but is not permitted into the quarantined zone … it feels like a romantic love story and could be 'read as such'. But Ellie is no simple Casanova cut-out. Obviously in this endless parade of possible quests, you are given the opportunity to aid Ellie in reaching her girl, or her 'friend', as she calls her with shifty eyes. First you have to complete a set of collection and disguise tasks. Mainly, grabbing an ID cartridge and sneaking about in restricted areas. It turns out later, things have soured between the women and money is owed.

Completing Ellie's quest means she can tag along with you when you have finished. Ellie is often heard making moody observations and getting into seemingly random fights with the other characters you collect in your spaceship's kitchen. She generally spends her time providing an enjoyable visual background of heartily pissed off gun-toting space butch swagger to whatever you are all getting up to in any given scene. She keeps her cards close to her chest however. Unlike with Parvati, you will find it is much harder to get her to open up about her side quests. She is particularly touchy on her parents, and it is not easy to find out more through conversation alone. She's generally a woman of few words, and short temper, on any major topic close to her heart or personal history. She doesn't particularly come out as gay but then, many video game dykons don't. To me her gender non-conforming aesthetic is pleasurable enough in adding some LGBTIQ+ diversity action on our screens and to some extent plays to the desire of gamers to interpret characters and messaging in games at will (Muriel & Crawford, 2020). She feels like a kind of space-bound K-Stew. By that I mean she would get more offended than Parvati if your character dared to prod into her sex life or force some sort of consistent narrative onto it. Fair enough.

Digital Intimacy Rating: 3/10.

Martin Callahan & Other Corporate Sheeple

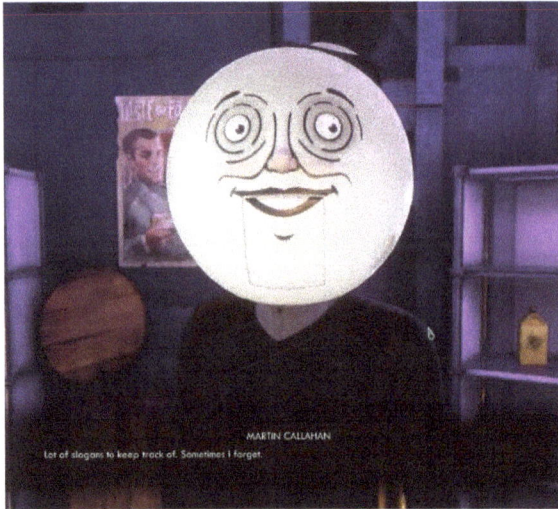

Outer Worlds is arguably also a game in which its creators at Obsidian are erecting their collective middle finger at corporations … which in the game appear to have claimed the giant's share of earnings, whilst pushing their employees to produce lesser quality products at an impossible pace. Long story short: the majority of planets and cities you can visit in *Outer Worlds* are either directly run by 'The Corporation' under 'The Board'. A small band of rebels or misfits, fight against said corporate machine's demands for their profits and increased efficiencies … often at a great cost to quality of life, length of life and life itself.

The people you encounter vary in their awareness of this corporation-slave dynamic and the revolutionary counter-cultures arising across the solar systems. They range from feeling a vigilante rage and pitching violent revolutionary rebellions against their corporate overseers like the anti-corporate Iconoclasts (whom you can join or lead with guns blazing); right through to feeling an irrational to-the-death loyalty to their employers. Some are literally working themselves early into their corporate-required graves after pre-paying their overseers' gravesite fees via their own endless labour. Arguably one of the most both comical, and sad, embodiments of the latter group is seen in the character Martin Callahan. You meet Callahan, an employee of the Spacer's Choice corporation whose own face is always obscured by his Moon-face Spacer's Choice Moon Man mascot helmet, on the independent ship Groundbreaker. He stands dejected at a shop where he is perpetually working as a vendor of a range of Spacer's Choice goods. He speaks with a notably exasperated voice when dealing with the player and will often ironically end dialogue lines with Spacer's Choice slogans like '*...it's not the best choice, it's Spacer's Choice*' and '*Taste the freedom*'. Callahan has extensive dialogue options that allow you to pry into the disturbing depths (or lack thereof) of the mindsets of corporate sheeple. Upon longer interrogations, you can attempt to subvert his thinking and see how well he responds.

Digital Intimacy Rating: 0+/10… how much time are you putting into this guy?

Conclusion

Overall, whilst it could come off as a generic shoot-'em game where at times you battle plenty of space creatures and robots, really *The Outer Worlds* is strongly affected by the choices you make and the intimacies you develop or reject. Especially, it is shaped by your choices in either aiding corporations or any of the many factions rebelling against them, aiming at various goals and levels of independence or revolution. This all plays on the increasing emphasis on creating a sense of the importance of player agency and intimacy in modern gaming design overall (Muriel & Crawford, 2020), particularly in the Massive Open World genre.

The strong focus on the choices made around asexual characters and queer companion options probably widens the accessibility to LGBTIQ+ content given the restrictions for gaming content around the globe, and the game considers romantic or companionship intimacies more than it does direct sexual contact … and particularly the issues of not wanting sexual contact. This is an innovation I personally welcome. The corporate geopolitics of the game take up more of the characters' headspace, as well as feelings of loyalty to people and ideas, than these factors might otherwise in a genre I find often associated with characters chasing sexual partners. You may not want to think about the commodification of your work or the structural domination of corporate entities in politics, geopolitics and even life and death. But this game will seep into your subconscious and directly make you choose whose side you are on, again and again and again. Until these questions are holistically faced. The thoroughness of the consequences for your stance in these virtual outer worlds, gives one pause when reflecting back on one's real-world life positions on capitalism and their long-term outcomes beyond the game.

References

Deluzio Chasin, C. (2011). Theoretical Issues in the Study of Asexuality. *Archives of Sexual Behavior, 40*(1), pp.713-716.

Emens, E. (2014). Compulsory sexuality: asexuality as means to broaden antidiscrimination law framework. *Stanford Law Review, 66*(2), pp.345-387.

Hillier, L., Jones, T., Monagle, M., Overton, N., Gahan, L., Blackman, J., & Mitchell, A. (2010). *Writing Themselves In 3: The Third National Study on the Sexual Health and Wellbeing of Same-sex Attracted and Gender Questioning Young People*. Retrieved from Melbourne: http://www.latrobe.edu.au/ssay/assets/downloads/wti3_web_sml.pdf

Jones, T., Hart, B., Carpenter, M., Ansara, G., Leonard, W., & Lucke, J. (2016). *Intersex: Stories and Statistics from Australia*. London: Open Book Publisher.

Jovanokski, N. (2017). *Digesting Femininities: the feminist politics of contemporary food culture*. Cham: Palgrave Macmillan.

Muriel, D., & Crawford, G. (2020). Video Games and Agency in Contemporary Society. *Games and Culture, 15*(2), pp.138-157.

Wrhel, N. (2017). *The Acest of Aces: Representations of Asexuality in Fiction*. (Masters of Arts in English). Truman State University, Kirksville Missouri.

Nessie Smith is an ace bi-romantic girl presently studying for a Bachelor of Arts. Besides enjoying student-life, Nessie loves gaming, cos-play events and writing. She wastes a lot of time on vehement 'next series' predication debates with strangers online who share her Sci Fi and Fantasy fandoms.

The Outer Worlds was developed by Obsidian Entertainment, and the images used here are gaming screen shots credited to Obsidian Entertainment. For more on the game visit: https://outerworlds.obsidian.net/en

D/s IN THE EVERYDAY
RAINICORN

Digital technologies and the dynamics of Dominance and submission

When we think about technology and sex, we most often think about sexting, cybering, or online pornography. We think about dating apps and websites that can fulfil our sexual fantasies. We think about sex robots and teledildonics, virtual reality porn and web-camming for unnamed audiences.

However, perhaps the greatest impact of digital technologies on people's sex lives has come from the enabling of global connection with communities that were once secret and hard to find. BDSM (Bondage and discipline, Dominance and submission, Sadism and masochism or sadomasochism), Fetish and/or Kink was once practiced in underground communities that were difficult to tap into. The internet has enabled access to spaces long kept secret.

The establishment of digital spaces such as Fetlife and Collarspace, reddit forums, fanfiction and blogs, and fetish websites have enabled widespread access to the underworld of BDSM, kink and fetish. BDSM is everywhere, from genres of literature, to featuring in music videos and influencing fashion. Technology has enabled engagement with BDSM on a global scale. Indeed, much can be said about BDSM and the digital world. Digital technologies have also enabled access to communities, to allow individuals to find BDSM, find a local kink or fetish event, or find someone who may share their desires. Such communities not only offer sexual play, but skill-sharing on safety, and techniques for engaging in what can be dangerous practices, such as impact play, Shibari (rope play), and needle play among others.

However, digital technology has not just allowed people greater access to kink communities and knowledge, it has become a tool in kink play itself. While there are many ways in which we can think about the entanglements of kink and technology, I want to focus more closely on one area, that is D/s (Dominance and submission) and technology.

What exactly is D/s?

D/s stands for Dominance and submission, in which two individuals (or more, if a Dominant chooses to have multiple submissives) take up agreed-upon roles in which one person has control (the Dominant), and the other submits to that control (the submissive) (Wiseman, 1993).

D/s can be a complex experience. It has many forms in many different kinds of relationships, and is sometimes considered a softer form of M/s (Master/slave), where the submissive may have more power to make conscious choices about what they choose to do or give up. D/s relationships may, or may not, include fetish and kink, impact, or other forms of pain or humiliation play.

The origins of D/s are somewhat difficult to trace, but can be linked all the way back to the ancient civilisation of Mesopotamia and the goddess worship of Inanna, in which she would whip her followers into sexual frenzies (O'Nomis, 2013). Elements of D/s can be found across time and cultures, across bodies, sexualities, and genders, and across varying kinds of kink and Fetish practices. D/s is a more recent variation of the BDSM practices of leather communities and others, which have long and transgressive queer histories (Weiss 2011; Damm et al., 2017).

My introduction to BDSM, was through the texts of the Marquis de Sade, sometimes known as the Father of Sadism. His philosophical contributions (*Philosophy in the Bedroom* (1795), *Justine* (1791), and *120 Days of Sodomy* (1785)) question the nature of humanity, the notion of 'original sin', and promote libertarian ideologies embedded in tales of sex, sadistic violence, Dominance and submission, carnality, and the grotesque. Another writer of influence is Leopold von Sacher-Masoch, the believed father of Masochism for his work *Venus in Furs* (1870). Elements of D/s, shrouded in pain as pleasure, can be noted throughout such texts. *The Story of O* (1954) by Anne Desclos is perhaps more indicative of the emotional and psychological aspects of submission, spurring the contemporary forms we see today. Indeed, films such as *The Secretary* (2002) provide a visualisation of what these relationships can be. Not only the sexual and the physical, but the emotional, mental, and spiritual elements.

When I talk about D/s, I am talking about how I personally understand, enact and engage it, but this is not necessarily an experience that others who engage in D/s dynamics will relate to. D/s is a personal experience, it holds different sets of meanings for different people. For me, D/s is the psychological, the emotional, the mental aspect of my kink. The things I do, the practices, are acts of submission, but to me, they are not submissive in and of themselves. Rather, it is the psychological and emotional meaning I attribute to such acts that render them a component of D/s.

This distinction, at least for me, is important. I do not see certain sexual acts as inherently dominant or submissive as others might. Being the receiver of anal sex, for example, is neutral to me. It is the meaning we ascribe that renders the act dominant or submissive, and that meaning can change depending on the dynamic of the relationship. Dominants may ask their submissives to service them sexually, and that may include acts of sex that might traditionally be seen as 'naturally' submissive—such as penetration. But to me, a Dom (male dominant), for example, is no less of a Dom if he enjoys a good pegging by his submissive. My point here is that submission, and Dominance, are a matter of mental framing They are not the act itself, but the meaning we personally ascribe, and that meaning can be fluid, flexible, and ever-changing.

Many people who practice D/s refer to their practices as 'In the Bedroom only' whereby D/s dynamics do not extend beyond a sexual play session and individuals return to 'vanilla' life on completion of the play.

But for myself, and for others, D/s is more than just bedroom play. It is a lifestyle, a way of life, often understood as 24/7 D/s or M/s. 24/7 denotes the acceptance of D/s dynamics in a more holistic sense, which can include not only sexual play, but everyday life activities that may, or may not, contain erotic elements. 24/7 D/s is about integrating D/s practice into 'everydayness'. Activities which may, to an outsider, seem banal or uninteresting become part of the D/s routine. Doing laundry. Cooking dinner. Tidying the house. These everyday activities may hold deeper meaning in D/s relationships.

Many people do not understand this dynamic. In conversations I have had with others, they contend that 24/7 is abusive, and that they would never engage or force their partner to engage in this practice. It can be hard to fully express the complexity of consciously giving up power and submitting to the whims of another, without this being seen as some form of abuse, like the bullshit depiction of D/s we saw in *50 Shades of Grey* (James, 2011) which involved manipulation and abuse. Dominance is also often misunderstood as exerting control without care for the consequences of those actions. But this is a misunderstanding. D/s is about the conscious and consensual giving over of control by the submissive, and the conscious taking of responsibility by the Dominant. It is about trust and deliberate power exchange. Those who engage in 24/7 dynamics do so with this understanding. It is complex and deep, and has spiritual, emotional, mental, and sexual elements.

Submission comes to me the more I feel engaged and trust someone, the more we communicate, the more I feel safe, valued, and loved. There is a feeling, or want, or desire, to give up power, rather than this being something that feels forced by someone.

For those of us deeply engaged in D/s dynamics, we recognise that the role of a Dominant is to care for, nurture, and guide a submissive through the exertion of control. That submissives must consent to any and all things done, and that there is love between the Dominant and submissive, what can be romantic, sexual, or platonic.

24/7 D/s is also often much more than a play session. It involves an on-going commitment, in which the submissive may be tasked and present themselves in an agreed upon set of ways for their Dominant. Such tasks may be or may not be sexual in nature, but are designed to stimulate submission. Non-sexual tasks may include domestic servitude, the running of errands, or they may involve longer-term forms of nurturing and development, such as going back to school to get a degree, or starting a new hobby, or engaging in health treatment. In return for their submission, the Dominant provides nurturing, assists the submissive to grow, to challenge themselves, and to push boundaries where appropriate.

Digital Technologies and The Everydayness of D/s

Digital technologies have enabled forms of Dominance and submission in interesting and transformative ways that go way beyond merely sending dirty text messages or videos that feature one showing off a new collar, or butt plug, or flogger. It is also much more than meeting up in chatrooms and forums and dating apps to facilitate D/s connections. Rather, mobile technology offers a range of diverse and creative ways to engage and maintain D/s connections. Some of the more obvious uses of technology for D/s are sexual in nature. The request to take an erotic photo or film an erotic act in a public place. Perhaps uploading photos of playscenes to fetish websites. Teledildonics, blue-tooth vibrators, vibrating cockrings and anal plugs that submissives can secretly wear in public while their Dominant controls the settings. Tech can be part of prolonged edging play, anal sex training, and orgasm control and denial.

But what about the less-talked about apps, the ones that enable D/s dynamics in ways that are not necessarily tied directly to sex, eroticism and pleasure? The ones that enable D/s play to become part of the everyday—the 24/7.

Digital technologies now allow someone to monitor and track multiple aspects of another person's life. Before I talk about the potential these technologies bring to D/s practices, it has to be noted that these technologies can also used to abuse and violate others. When I speak about the use of technology in D/s play, I am talking about deliberate, consensual use of technology within the context of a mutually trusting relationship. This is the essence of D/s. Trust is what enables one to relinquish power.

In the first instance, the simplicity of instant messaging, whether it's through a mobile app or social media platform, or just SMS, allows for the presence of D/s even if Dominants and submissives do not live together. Text makes it easy for a Dominant to send a quick message to a submissive to task them, for a submissive to request permission to do a certain activity, or uphold certain practices of communication. With my current Dom, we always text good morning and good night, regardless of where we are in the world. This might mean He receives a good morning text at some odd time if I'm travelling overseas for work. This seems ordinary, and simple, yet this practice is one that maintains a strong presence of D/s even though we live apart, and with different primary partners. [A cautionary tale. I have made the embarrassing mistake of sending a request for permission text to not a former Dominant, but to two work colleagues! Fortunately, they were understanding].

Mobile geo-tracking apps can be used to ensure submissives are where they should be. There is an underlying eroticism knowing that your Dominant can see where you are, the honesty demanded of you. Some may even use this as forms of permission, 'Sir/Mistress, may I leave to go for a walk?' and so forth. As the nights grow darker in winter, my Dom can follow my walk to ensure I get safely home. While I was introduced to this form of control in a D/s capacity, I have adapted this with non-D/s polyamorous partners to ensure safety when meeting new people.

For Dominants who enjoy dressing, choosing, or approving clothing choices, clothing organisation apps allow submissives to create outfits and send photos for approval. Indeed, some apps allow multiple logins, meaning that Dominants can choose outfits for their submissives, and suggest items for purchase. Submissives may be tasked to take photos of their outfits each day to prove they are wearing what has been approved, or even just when meeting up with Dominants.

For submissives who have requested support in fitness, health, and nutrition regimes, apps such as fitness trackers and watches, can be used to monitor their progress, and check-in if progress falters. Some of these also allow for multiple logins, meaning that Dominants can login to provide support and encouragement. This may extend to mental health apps that support the tracking of mental health, so Dominants can support submissives on days when they are experiencing poorer mental health, or remind them to engage in mindfulness and self-coping activities. I myself have a long-standing habit of not drinking enough water, and often being dehydrated as a result. A water-tracking app has been useful to 'prove' a change of habit to my Dom by tracking my water consumption. This has enabled a shift in habit where I actively work to ensure I drink enough water.

For submissives who menstruate, period-tracking apps may also be useful for planning sexual activities if blood play is a limit, or in some cases, desired. For submissives whose Dominants are more involved in the daily management of their health, medication tracking apps may also be utilised to support health and medical treatment.

Online project management tools, or list-type apps, can be a space in which Dominants can organise tasks for their submissives to be completed within a timeframe, and to help both the Dominant and the submissive keep track of what has been agreed. My Dom and I have even used these tools to quickly note topics of conversation if there are any concerns that need to be addressed the next time we see each other in person. This ensures our conversations remain on point, and has enabled a deeper form of trust and communication.

Diary writing or journal entries are important ways in which submissives and Dominants can connect. Submissives may be tasked with writing a journal that can assist the Dominant in having a better understanding of their wants, needs, and desires, as well as if things are not working for them. Blogging tools such as Wordpress or Tumblr, set to private, can be spaces in which submissives can share inner thoughts, ideas, and feelings. Of course, shared calendars may be vital between Dominants and submissives, particularly those with multiple partners or play-dates, and those who live apart and maintain busy working lives.

My point here is that digital technologies enable an everydayness of D/s that is vital for ongoing 24/7 dynamics. Activities that are ordinary and banal, hold an entirely different set of meanings for those participating in D/s. Yet as Lefebreve and Levich (1987) would contend, the everyday is extraordinary in its own right.

> Banality? Why should the study of the banal itself be banal? Are not the surreal, the extraordinary, the surprising, even the magical, also part of the real? Why wouldn't the concept of everydayness reveal the extraordinary in the ordinary?

Many of the practices I describe may seem uninteresting, and yet for me, and others, they hold significant meaning, and are indicative of trust and the conscious decision of giving and taking power in a D/s dynamic. The use of such technologies for practices that for many are dark, mysterious, and taboo, reveal the extraordinary in the banality of our lives.

References

Damm, Cassandra., Dentato, Michael P., & Busch, Nikki. (2018). Unravelling intersecting identities: understanding the lives of people who practice BDSM, *Psychology & Sexuality*, 9:1, 21-37.

Desclos, Anne. (1954). *The Story of O*. London, UK: Penguin (Classics) Publishers.

De Sade, Marquis. (1785). *120 Days of Sodomy*. London, UK: Penguin (Classics) Publishers.

De Sade, Marquis. (1791). *Justine*. London, UK: Penguin (Classics) Publishers.

De Sade, Marquis. (1795). *Philosophy in the Bedroom*. London, UK: Penguin (Classics) Publishers.

James, E.L. (2011). *Fifty Shades of Grey*. New York, UK: Vintage Books.

Lefebvre, H., & Levich, C. (1987). The Everyday and Everydayness. *Yale French Studies*, (73), 7-11.

O'Nomis, Anne. (2013). *The History & Arts of the Dominatrix*. Melbourne, AU: Ebook Partnership.

von Sacher-Masoch, Leopold. (1870). *Venus in Furs*. London, UK: Penguin (Classics) Publishers.

Weiss, Margot. (2011). *Techniques of Pleasure: BDSM and the Circuits of Sexuality*. Durham, NC: Duke University Press.

Wiseman, Jay. (1993). *S&M 101: A Realistic Introduction*. Emeryville, CA: Greenery Press.

Rainicorn works in research, focusing on bodies, sexuality and gender, sexual practices, and health and well-being. She identifies as a bisexual, cisgender, polyamorous plus-size Anglo-Celtic woman, and is sex positive, kink/fetish positive, and fat positive. In her spare time, she enjoys painting and composing music, and the delectable delights of the carnal underworld.

LIFE, BUT NOT AS WE KNOW IT
GEOFF ALLSHORN

Star Trek, fan culture, slash fiction and the queering of Starfleet Command

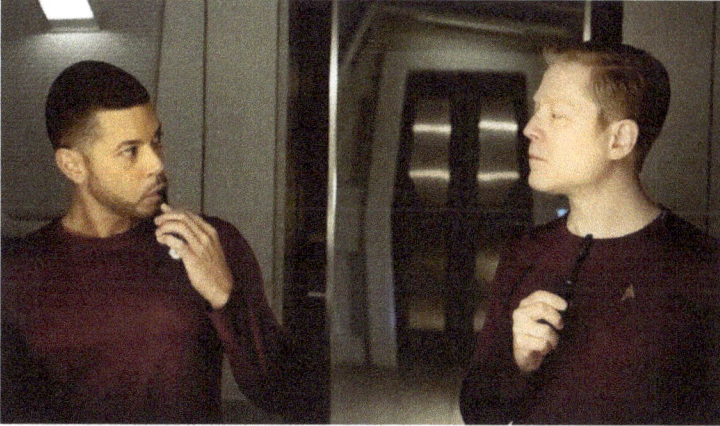

'Beam Me Up, Scotty!'

Many will immediately recognise this catchphrase as a testimony to nerd culture and cult television. Yet in its day, it was a somewhat covert signal between adherents in much the same way as talking about being 'a friend of Dorothy' indicated membership of another fringe group.

When considering how technology has transformed social norms regarding sexuality and intimacy, we might think most readily of Grindr, social media, and even more ubiquitous tech such as mobile phones and the Internet. My story begins before any of this technology existed, back in the days of what may now be considered dinosaur tech, such as free-to-air television, the typewriter, the fordigraph machine, and the film camera. This now-outdated tech helped plug me into a Matrix of alternate reality that introduced me to my first 'out' gay, lesbian, bisexual, trans and queer friends, in an era when male homosexuality was still illegal and LGBT people were shunned by polite society. This dinosaur tech also introduced me to a counter-culture of bohemian people whose lifestyles and views were open expressions of inclusion, diversity and difference.

Television

There was a time when the apex of popular communication technology in Australia was free-to-air colour television, comprising a standalone box with an antenna. There were no videotapes or DVDs, no satellite or cable TV, no streaming or iTunes, so viewers relied totally upon the whims of local TV station programmers for whatever content they might get to view. Those seeking other visual entertainment could go to the local movie cinema.

Amidst the cultural fare of programs like *The Beverley Hillbillies*, *Are You Being Served?* and *The Paul Hogan Show,* my young teenage self sought somewhat higher inspiration and aspiration. I found the world of *Star Trek*. It was a wondrous place, filled with spaceships and aliens, diverse peoples and galactic technological marvels. Although it offered no explicitly queer themes or characters, its variety of aliens implicitly endorsed the principles of diversity and inclusion. The addition of the half-human, half-Vulcan character, Spock, was also extremely popular with audiences, with many people admiring different aspects of his complex character. Stephen Fry asserts the Spock character to be a Nietzschean counterbalance to his two closest human associates as a symbolic representation of different aspects of the human psyche (Knight, 2010). Barbara Jacobs has even suggested that Spock serves as a possible role model for those with Asperger's Syndrome (Jacobs, 2003, 38); while SF author Joanna Russ explores the idea that 'Spock is a woman' in that he displays attributes or characteristics that were common to gender expectations for women in earlier times—cyclical and uncontrollable sexuality, a submissive and subservient nature, etc (Russ, 1985, 29). This gender subversion would arguably become important within a cultural phenomenon that I will discuss shortly.

Many fans upheld Spock as an archetype in that he embodied optimism amidst the universal human condition of loneliness: 'This is an optimism that says it is *possible* to find somebody who understands your innermost silent and lonely battles' (Lichtenberg et al, 1975,101). Such sensitivities within the character appear to have come directly from the background of *Star Trek* creator, Gene Roddenberry, who spoke of his childhood as a time when he felt different and isolated (Roddenberry, 1976). The universal nature of Spock's inner conflicts: balancing logic with emotion, and alien with human, led one *Star Trek* analyst to declare that, 'We Are All Spock' (Blair, 1977,160). He became popular among many adolescents such as myself, who were seeking a role model as a metaphoric *other* exploring the strange new world of adult life. Added layers of nuance within his character were undoubtedly familiar to young LGBT kids in my day: being someone who was 'emotionally guarded' and living a life that testifies: 'it's no big jump from alien to alienated...' (Russ, 1985, 29). In a 2015 fan eulogy for the actor Leonard Nimoy, I wrote of his character's significance in my own life some decades earlier, when I had faced stigma, prejudice and discrimination:

> Spock was a kindred spirit, someone who had found strength, pride and nobility in being different ... Spock's resilience and quiet dignity in the face of intolerance, or bullying, or alien dangers; served as an example to ennoble and enable the lives of many fans who might otherwise have felt isolation or despair. (Allshorn, 2015, 13)

Star Trek was a utopian fantasy that explored galaxies of diverse ideas. While Australia was grappling with the idea of multiculturalism in the 1970s, I was absorbing the *Star Trek* philosophy of *Infinite Diversity in Infinite Combinations* (*IDIC*). The *Star Trek* fan base has always been welcoming of those whom normal society might consider to be aliens in our midst. *Star Trek* actor and LGBT activist George Takei elaborates on this conjoining of diversity with inclusion: 'The show always appealed to people that were different — the geeks and the nerds, and the people who felt they were not quite a part of society, sometimes because they may have been gay or lesbian' (Lang, 2015). Even after *Star Trek's* popularity had peaked, it was reported that *Star Trek Voyager* was equal third most popular TV show (alongside *The Simpsons*) in San Francisco (PlanetOut staff, 2000). LGBT viewers have always been attracted to this TV program—even though its implied diversity has not explicitly included queer characters or themes—and they have been prepared to translate its sense of inclusion into real life.

As part of this inclusive mindset, enthusiastic fans sent letters to the *Star Trek* offices offering constructive suggestions for future *Star Trek* adventures. Among their suggestions back in the early days of gay liberation was a request that gay characters be included in order to demonstrate and promote tolerance (Sackett, 1977, 166). This call was ignored by *Star Trek* creators, so the fans created their own reality. They took ideas from television and translated them into real life.

Typewriters and Fordigraph Machines

Star Trek fandom attracted a large influx of female authors and participants, indicating that something specific within *Star Trek* must have attracted the interest and passion of such women. Part of the attraction, it seems, was an interest in what became known as the Kirk/Spock relationship. This was possibly first glimpsed in a 1967 episode of *Star Trek* called *Amok Time*, which featured exotic Vulcan (hetero)sexuality with just a hint of homo-suggestive entanglement. (*Sinclair, J. and D'Anne, eds*, 2016).

Eager for more *Star Trek* adventures, fans wrote their own. Female *Star Trek* fans grabbed their typewriters and fordigraph (or similar hand-operated spirit duplicator) machines to assertively self-publish fan fiction ('fanfic' or 'fic') stories within amateur fan magazines ('fanzines' or 'zines'). Actor Leonard Nimoy acknowledged the popularity of heterosexual fanfic written by these women, whose zines ranged from generic *Star Trek* stories to others that were outright erotic—some of which transgressed beyond heterosexuality into the homoerotic:

> The cover of one of these 'fan-zines' in particular shows `a very well done drawing of Mr Spock stripped to the waist, his lower portion covered for the most part with a draped toga exposing one bare leg, his hands manacled and a belt from the manacles chaining him to a post. The title boldly reads 'Spock Enslaved!' The obvious suggestion is that Spock in this case is a love slave, much in the same way that women have been used for years in erotic or semi-erotic literature. I suppose in this case, turn about is fair play. (Nimoy, 1975, 55)

Expanding upon this idea, heterosexual Australian fan Diane Marchant wrote a story entitled *A Fragment Out of Time,* which was published in a 1974 issue of an adult US *Star Trek* fanzine called *Grup* (Roberts, 2015). Her story is widely recognised as being the first zine-published slash story (so-named after the coded slash symbol in 'K/S' being shorthand for 'Kirk/Spock'), although there are other claimants to the actual origins of slash (fanlore, 2020b). The slash symbol refers to stories containing what became popularly known as 'the premise', that is the practice of taking established or potential character relationships and extending them into deeper same-sex attraction (fanlore, 2020 b & d). Diane was a friend and mentor of mine, and I know that her reticence to identify Kirk and Spock within her story—and her reluctance to ever talk about it—reflected a lifelong sensitivity regarding material which may create contention, friction or scandal, evocative of the era when '… gay relationships of any variety, even fictional, were considered deviant, overtly sexual and perverted' (Smith, 2018). Nonetheless, the precedent she set, and the aspects of *Star Trek* fandom that arose in response, gave women an avenue for expression of ideas which were, for their time, quite unconventional:

> As the first depiction of a love scene between Kirk and Spock, it wasn't just hot; it was a way of making visible the thread of attraction that runs through the complex bond between the two characters. It elevated subtext to text. In doing so it gave rise to an entire writhing, sweating universe of romantic and sexual pairings. But slash isn't just about making porn out of things that weren't already porn. It's also about prosecuting fanfiction's larger project of breaking rules and boundaries and taboos of all kinds. (Grossman, 2013).

In the historical context, the burgeoning female fan movement helped to provide women with liberated and liberating expressions of recognition, sexuality and empowerment, and many chose this freedom to lend support to other marginalised forms of sexual or gender identity. They also expanded their scope to other science fiction and TV/literary identities: *Blake's Seven*, *Starsky and Hutch*, *Babylon 5*, and many others. However, slash as a genre is not without its potential problems: 'Slash is important in creating queer representation; it's fun and pleasurable for many people and that's important too; but slash can sometimes be regressive, sexist, or fetishizing.' (Flourish, 2017).

As a young gay man, I personally never found slash fiction to be particularly appealing or authentic to my life. I concluded that slash was not exploring the gay experience so much as it was presenting women's fantasies of idealised romantic/sexual love liberated from oppressive patriarchal and homophobic traditions. In my day, slash was believed to be the purview of predominantly heterosexual women, but later fan media discourse began to recognise the presence of LGBT authors and readers (NB, 1992) and then go beyond the gay/straight binary into fuller recognition of a spectrum of 'queer' identities (Lackner et al, 2006, 193—4). By the early 2000s, women had greater freedoms to 'come out' than they had in earlier decades and this has led to the increased visibility of LGBT people: 'Anecdotal evidence and informal polls suggest that the number of not-straight women is proportionately higher in fandom than in the population at large' (Busse, 2006, 208).

This female fan cohort may have actually resuscitated and saved the *Star Trek* franchise (McNally, 2016) and forever changed the gender ratio within the science fiction community. Many of these women became prominent in *Star Trek* and science fiction clubs, convention committees and fanzines, reshaping the role of women in such community activism. The number of *Star Trek* clubs and fanzine titles worldwide peaked at approximately 450 each in 1977 (Verba 2003, 35). These fanzines—predominantly written, illustrated, edited and read by women—were often comprised of multiple issues of adult or slash content. This helped to not only promote female self-empowerment, but their gender subversion included voluntary exploration of non-heterosexist, liberated, erotic, subversive, female-directed, queer-normative literature:

> Many fans took it upon themselves to read more into the Kirk/Spock relationship than had ever been hinted at on screen. In the early days of fanzines, some were dedicated to amateur fan stories that explored various facets of this non-canonical relationship. This was never recognised on screen, and in general Star Trek has been heavily criticised for its relative failure—at a time when the television landscape was becoming even more diverse—to depict lesbian, gay, bisexual or transgender (LGBT) characters or to craft stories dealing with the issues of LGBT rights … (Robb, 2012, 184).

Now long superseded by digital publishing, paper fanzines have gone the way of other dinosaur tech and been replaced by online fanfic repositories such as http://www.archiveofourown.org/. Slash also proliferates on the Internet via apps such as Pinterest and Instagram. Meanwhile, fanfic continues to grow (Joyce, 2016). The *Star Trek* franchise has never officially acknowledged the role of these fans, nor the immense marketing potential of slash or other fanfic.

New Tech, New Trek

Star Trek fans have always been at the forefront of using or adapting technology. For their originally rudimentary forms of costumed roleplay (cosplay), they created costumes out of velour and glitter and papier-mâché and tinfoil, and cobbled together props out of whatever was at hand; they recorded episodes on audio cassettes. For social networking and *Star Trek* news, they might join a local club and await its fordigraphed monthly newsletter. Those wanting international networking generally relied on the snail-mail postal service (and maybe an occasional operator-assisted overseas phone call from their home phone). International pen-pal (and free holiday visit) networks sprang up around the world. This tendency to innovate and reinvent led many fan authors, artists, scientists, computer wizards, astronauts, medical specialists and others to change the world with new ideas and tech ranging from medical scanners to mobile phones (Evangelista, 2004; Handel & Jones, 2005).

In the early 1970s, after the original *Star Trek* had been cancelled, the explosive growth of paper fanzines helped to revive the franchise, until their eventual demise in the 1990s. More recently, during the early years of the 21st century, fans once again began to reclaim the temporarily-stalled franchise through their increasing use of more modern technology: fan films. Such films have been around since at least 1974 (Wikipedia, 2020) and Melbourne's own local *Star Trek* club, Austrek, produced its own fan films in 1979 and 1993 (Maxwell, 2017?), but the arrival of digital technology led to an explosion of fan films on the Internet from the early 2000s onwards.

One fan film series, *Star Trek: Hidden Frontier*, included gay characters and queer outer space romances that were treated with the same acceptance that the original *Star Trek* extended towards heterosexuality. One episode even featured *Star Trek*'s first openly, out-and-proud gay on-screen kiss (Hidden Frontier, 2004)—not a relationship layered in metaphor (Wong, 2018).

Another fan film series, *Star Trek: New Voyages*, featured a two-part story that gave *Star Trek* writer, David Gerrold, the chance to revisit his

Blood and Fire episode which had been rejected by *Star Trek* back in the 1980s. The story featured a gay couple and allegorised the AIDS epidemic which was at its height when the script was originally written. One commentator spoke with hope about the optimism inherent in such fan films and within *Star Trek* in general:

> … its central theme of a future where mankind actually gets along no matter what our race, gender, age, hairline, or even species is a very positive one that I think appeals to a gay audience. (Cross, 2007).

Once again, fan fiction would precede the franchise in promoting LGBT rights.

I have been, and always shall be, your friend

The *Star Trek* franchise has a long history of homophobia and LGBT erasure (Sinclair,, 2003). Although modern-day audiences today often interpret older episodes or characters to be queer-supportive or queer-friendly (Hennessy, 2019), an analysis of these same characters and allegories within their contemporaneous settings reveals heteronormativity and covert homophobic insinuation (Ex Astris Scientia, 2020; McNally, 2020). Conversely, *Star Trek* has been appropriated by its legions of LGBT and other followers—if not in a strictly legal copyright sense, then certainly as a source of intellectual and philosophical inspiration. Although the franchise has avoided LGBT characters and stories—prompting one Australian LGBT commentator to lament: '… there are no poofs and no dykes in the future' (McKee, 1996, 13)—the LGBT community and slash supporters continue to be fascinated by the implied diversity in its fantasies. It is interesting to see how *Star Trek* as a Hollywood franchise has evolved—or not—in response to this social evolution.

In 1979, the novelisation of the first official *Star Trek* movie contained a cautiously coded reference to slash fiction by acknowledging the Kirk/Spock relationship as being *t'hy'la*—somehow more than brothers but less than lovers—and firmly rebutting any suggestion of sexual interaction (Roddenberry, 1979, 18 & 19). Subsequent *Star Trek* movies toyed with coded gay comic references ('Please, Jim, not in front of the Klingons') and in 2016, the most recent *Star Trek* film contained an acknowledgement of the character Sulu being gay in a scene that actor George Takei described as, 'If you blinked, you missed it' (Kooser, 2016). The most recent *Star Trek* shows, *Discovery* and *Picard* have somewhat reluctantly begun including LGBT characters but still cannot not resist deferring to problematic old *Star Trek* tropes such as killing off their queer characters (Duffy, 2018; Diaz, 2019; Opie, 2020). The *Star Trek* franchise—one that proclaims itself to 'boldly go where no one has gone before'—is still struggling to be out and proud, falling behind any number of other television and film franchises, over fifty years after its tech-savvy LGBT-friendly fan base built an inclusive community of queer-friendly bohemians and others who not only proclaimed diversity, but actually lived it. These pioneers are heroes in the history of LGBT civil rights; may their memory live long and prosper.

The author wishes to thank Dr Mirna Cicioni for her assistance with this article.

References

Allshorn, G. (2015). "I have been, and always shall be, your friend': A Tribute to Leonard Nimoy 1931—2015', *Captain's Log*, Austrek, May, 12—13.

Blair, K. (1977). *Meaning in Star Trek*, New York: Warner Books.

Busse, K. (2006). 'My Life Is a WIP on My LJ', in Karen Hellekson and Kristina Busse (eds.), *Fan Fiction and the Fan Communities in the Age of the Internet*, London: Mcfarland, 207-224.

Cross, D. (2007). Quoted in Stewart Who?, Gay.com/U.K, 'Star Trek Goes Gay', *Advocate*, 17 to 19 March, https://web.archive.org/web/20070320091406/https://www.advocate.com/news_detail_ektid43052.asp.

Diaz, E. (2019). 'STAR TREK: DISCOVERY Just Fixed Its Biggest Mistake', *Nerdist*, 15 February, https://nerdist.com/article/star-trek-discovery-gay-couple-back-to-life/

Duffy, N. (2018). 'There was a major twist on Star Trek: Discovery and gay fans are pissed off', *Pink News*, 8 January, https://www.pinknews.co.uk/2018/01/08/there-was-a-major-twist-on-star-trek-discovery-and-gay-fans-are-pissed-off/

Evangelista, B. (2004) 'TREK TECH / 40 years since the Enterprise's inception, some of its science fiction gadgets are part of everyday life', *San Francisco Chronicle*, 15 March, http://www.sfgate.com/cgi-bin/article.cgi?f=/chronicle/archive/2004/03/15/BUGO35EG1T83.DTL.

Ex Astris Scientia. (2020). 'Homosexuality in Star Trek', *Ex Astris Scientia*, https://www.ex-astris-scientia.org/inconsistencies/homosexuality.htm.

Fanlore. (2019). Main page, edit dated 20 January, https://fanlore.org/wiki/Main_Page

Fanlore. (2020a). 'Another Addict Raves About K/S', edit dated 1 March, https://fanlore.org/wiki/Another_Addict_Raves_About_K/S

= = = = (2020b). 'Kirk/Spock (TOS)', edit dated 20 May, https://fanlore.org/wiki/Kirk/Spock_(TOS)

= = = = (2020c). 'Nome (Star Trek: TOS zine published in the US)', edit dated 25 February, https://fanlore.org/wiki/Nome_(Star_Trek:_TOS_zine_published_in_the_ US)

= = = = (2020d). 'Slash', edit dated 30 January, https://fanlore.org/wiki/Slash

Flourish, E. (2017). Interviewed in Henry Jenkins (editor) & William Proctor (Associate Editor), 'The Multiplicity and Diversity of Fandom: An Interview with Fansplaining's Flourish Klink and Elizabeth Minkel (Part Three), *Henry Jenkins: Confessions of an ACA-Fan*, 12 December, http://henryjenkins.org/blog/2017/11/29/an-interview-with-fansplainings-flourish-klink-and-elizabeth-minkel-part-three

Gonzalez, C. (2010). 'Stephen Fry and Jennifer Byrne Q&A', in *Stephen Fry Live at the Sydney Opera House*, ABC DVD, Australian Broadcasting Corporation and Sydney Opera House.

Grossman, L. (2013). 'Foreword', in Anne Jamison, *Fic: Why Fanfiction Is Taking Over the World*, (Kindle edition), Texas: BenBella Books.

Handel, A. & Jones, J. (2005). *How William Shatner Changed the World*, Handel Productions (ST) Inc.

Harvey, E. (2018). 'The A. Bertram Chandler Award: What Goes Around Comes Around', in Bruce Gillespie (ed. & pub.), *Science Fiction Commentary #97*, August, 9—15.

Hennessy, C. (2019). '8 Reasons to Watch DS9 During Pride Month', *StarTrek.com*, 18 June, https://intl.startrek.com/news/8-reasons-to-watch-ds9-during-pride-month.

Hidden Frontier. (2004). 'CROSSROADS: Star Trek: Hidden Frontier—Episode 4.05', http://www.hiddenfrontier.net/works/hf405/.

Jacobs, B. (2003). *Loving Mr Spock: The Story of A Difference Kind of Love*, London: Michael Joseph/Penguin.

Joyce, H. (2016). 'To Boldly Go...', *The Economist*, August/September, https://www.1843magazine.com/features/to-boldly-go.

Kooser, A. (2016). 'George Takei calls 'Star Trek Beyond' gay Sulu scene 'a whisper'', CNET, 5 August, https://www.cnet.com/news/george-takei-calls-star-trek-beyond-gay-sulu-scene-a-whisper/

Lane, J. (2019). 'The very FIRST Star Trek fan film ever to be SHUT DOWN by the studio lawyers was in…1968???', Axanar, 8 September, https://axanar.com/the-very-first-star-trek-fan-film-ever-to-be-shut-down-by-the-studio-lawyers-was-in1968/.

Lackner, E; Lucas, BE; Reid, RA. (2006), 'Cunning Linguists. The Bisexual Erotics of *Words/Silence/Flesh*', in Karen Hellekson and Kristina Busse (eds.), *Fan Fiction and the Fan Communities in the Age of the Internet*, London: Mcfarland, 189-206.

Lang, B. (2015) 'George Takei on Same-Sex Marriage, Why 'Star Trek' Fans Are Gay Friendly, *Variety*, 26 June, https://variety.com/2015/film/news/george-takei-same-sex-marriage-1201529072/.

Lichtenberg, J; Marshak, S; Winston, J. (1975). *Star Trek Lives!*, New York: Bantam.

Maxwell, D. (2017?). 'The History of Austrek—How It All Began', *Austrek*, http://www.austrek.org/austrek-history.html

McKee, A. (1996). 'Star Trek Voyeur', *Brother Sister Issue #105*, 2 May.

McNally, V. (2016). 'Women who love 'Star Trek' are the reason that modern fandom exists', *Revelist*, 8 September, https://www.revelist.com/tv/star-trek-fandom-50th/4643.

McNally, V. (2020). 'Your Guide to Queer Identity and Metaphor in Star Trek', *StarTrek.Com*, 1 July, https://intl.startrek.com/news/your-guide-to-queer-identity-and-metaphor-in-star-trek.

Miller, S. M. (2017). ''Star Trek: Discovery' Cast and Crew: If You Don't Understand Diversity, You Don't Understand 'Star Trek'', *Indie Wire*, 22 July, https://www.indiewire.com/2017/07/star-trek-discovery-diversity-backlash-sonequa-martin-green-1201858861/.

NB. (1992). Quoted in 'Camille Bacon-Smith and Henry Jenkins at Gaylaxicon 1992 (Part Two)', in Henry Jenkins (editor) & William Proctor (Associate Editor), *Henry Jenkins: Confessions of an ACA-Fan*, 24 February 2010, http://henryjenkins.org/blog/2010/02/camille_bacon-smith_and_henry.html

Nimoy, L. (1975). *I Am Not Spock*, Millbrae: Celestial Arts.

Opie, D. (2020). 'Star Trek: Picard missed an opportunity to correct Discovery's big mistake', *Digital Spy*, 28 January, https://www.digitalspy.com/tv/ustv/a30655664/star-trek-picard-lgbtq-gay-queer-discovery-interview/

PlanetOut staff. (2000). 'Gay TV Viewing Habits', *PlanetOut*, 24 November.

Robb, BJ. (2012) *Star Trek: The Essential History of the Classic TV Series and the Movies*, Constable & Robinson/Running Press.

Roberts, TR. (2015). 'Diane Marchant & Kirk/Spock [SF Women of the 20th Century]', tansyrr.com, 26 August, http://tansyrr.com/tansywp/2-diane-marchant-kirkspock-sf-women-of-the-20th-century/

Roddenberry, G. (1976). 'The Star Trek Dream', *Inside Star Trek*, Columbia Records, July; reissued in the 1999 two-CD set, *Star Trek: The Motion Picture—20th Anniversary Collector's Edition*. See also https://memory-alpha.fandom.com/wiki/Inside_Star_Trek.

= = = = = = = = (1979). *Star Trek—The Motion Picture*, London: Futura Publications.

Russ, J. (1985). 'Another Addict Raves about K/S', in Victoria Clark and Barbara L. Storey (eds.), *NOME #8*, May, 27—37. Note that Russ credits Dr Patricia Frazer Lamb with the idea that, 'Spock is a woman'. Note that the editors of this publication were identified in *fanlore* and those related web pages (fanlore, 2020 a & c) are also listed in this reference section.

Sackett, S. (1977). *Letters to Star Trek*, New York: Ballantine Books.

Sinclair, David. (2003). *Gay, Lesbian & Bisexual Characters on Star Trek,* https://web.archive.org/web/20080831083404/http://www.webpan.com/dsinclair/trek.html

Sinclair, J. and D'Anne (eds.). (2016). Short History of Kirk/Spock Slash, 15 October, http://www.beyonddreamspress.com/history.htm.

Smith, A. (2018). 'A 50-year Trekkie bestows *Star Trek* history upon the next generation: How fandom and fanfiction sparked the galaxy's most controversial romance', 8 August, *Colorado Springs Indy,* https://www.csindy.com/coloradosprings/a-50-year-trekkie-bestows-star-trek-history-upon-the-next-generation-how-fandom-and-fanfiction-sparked-the-galaxys-most-controversial-romanc/Content?oid=14273176.

Takei, G. (2004). *To the Stars: The Autobiography of George Takei*, New York: Pocket Books.

Verba, JM. (2003). *Boldly Writing: A Trekker Fan and Zine History 1967—1987*, 2nd edition, Minneapolis: FTL Publications.

Wikipedia. (2020). 'Star Trek fan productions', *Wikipedia*, edit dated 19 June, https://en.wikipedia.org/wiki/Star_Trek_fan_productions.

Wong, CM. (2018), 'How 'Star Trek' Made History 22 Years Ago With A Same-Sex Kiss', *Huffpost*, 4 March, https://www.huffingtonpost.com.au/entry/star-trek-lesbian-kiss_n_5abea3d8e4b0a47437aafd92?ri18n=true.

Geoff Allshorn is a former schoolteacher who has recently been undertaking postgraduate research on the history of HIV/AIDS. He has been a member of many LGBT and other community/activist groups, and has received a number of awards relating to this activism.

VIRAL LESBIANS
TIFFANY JONES

Geopolitical uses of digital meme worship and sharing

Dear Corona-Chan, you're so beautiful I can hardly breathe even without your disease....

Many memes on the Coronavirus are circulating the internet. Trump's misinformation, including his recommendation to explore injecting or drinking disinfectants, might seem the worst virus-related memes being copy-pasted and shared in 2020. Or perhaps his advice to take untested drugs his family has financial ties to … However, far more sinister viral virus disinformation memes are in distribution. Of those, the ones explored in this article are more subtle and effective. They are aimed at larger goals than simply lining Trump family pockets, including attempts at disrupting global orders for cyberwar related functions. Viruses are being anthropomorphised—attributed human-like forms and traits—to spread geopolitical conspiracy theories on social media. As is often the case, highly sexualised LGBTIQ+ identities are being exploited to help make these memes spread faster, and to ensure they more deeply penetrate the collective psyche. This article considers the new phenomenon of the 'viral lesbian virus waifu', and her use in cyberwarfare.

Waifus: Fictional Digital Intimates

'Waifu' is a term for a favoured fictional woman. It is taken from a Japanese katakana spelling for the English word 'wife' (Bailey & Harvey, 2019). Waifus are understood as characters one feels a special sexual and/or romantic attraction to. The use of the Japanese term is due to the strong association with and prevalence of 'waifu worship' in Japanese anime and digital character fan subcultures. People who love, or are attracted, to one or more waifus may for example:

- collect their waifus' images,
- engage in sexual fantasies about their waifus,
- discuss or depict their waifus with a fervor on online discussion-boards and social media postings, and/or
- engage in acts related to the fantasies about the waifus, alone or with waifu-related merchandise, costumes (cos-play), or partners.

These expressions can be harmless enough. However they can broadly be associated with frustrations that attest to waifus' simultaneous attractiveness and unreality… 'waifus are desirable, but are always out of reach' (Bailey & Harvey, 2019, p. 332).

Waifu admirers may see themselves as having failed to engage in romantic relationships, quitting the heterosexual romantic economy, and/or living out a 'nerdy/geeky' identity or failed masculinity (Kendall, 2002). By sexualizing fictional non-human characters, especially where associated with children's anime genres or other cartoon programs for example, waifu lovers can also be seen to trespass standard boundaries of 'good and bad sex' (Rubin, 2013). Online communities worshipping waifus may facilitate not only stigmatised identities, but thus also the emergence of a communal politics that emphasises economic and sexual failing (the inabilities to get jobs and partners), shame and anxieties in ways leading to a sense of *collective sexual disadvantage* and *reliance on the online community for support* (Bailey & Harvey, 2019). In this sense, waifu worship communities can become relatively closed and passionate worlds with tribalized cultures strongly influencing their members.

Ebola-Chan: Viral White Lesbian Nurse Waifu

One example of a viral virus waifu is 2014+ meme 'Ebola-chan'. She is a Caucasian-stylised character with wide innocent golden-brown eyes, little purple demon wings and a permanently happy disposition. She is usually pictured wearing pink pigtails curling into worm-like ebola virus shapes and a clinging white nurse outfit, holding a bloody skull or posing in sexually available ways in a bloody room or with various lesbian lovers. She was designed as a female anime representation of the ebola virus and cited to social media application pixiv user 'sly' on August 4th 2014. Shortly after an image macro in Figure 1 began circulating on 4chan boards featuring the same anime character sketch comment with a caption calling her 'Ebola-chan', urging readers to reply with 'I Love You Ebola-chan' on the discussion-board to avoid contracting a painful, fatal disease (Kaufman, 2014; Kharel, 2014).

The meme was shared, reblogged and changed across a multitude of sites including Cheezburger site Geek Universe, Reddit, and deviantART. The meme was used to spread the conspiracy theory that says Ebola-Chan virus was deliberately created by Western countries or the US CIA using black magic and rituals, or biological warfare, to harm African people. The theory is particularly popular on Nigerian websites; including the forum 'Nairaland' where users commented in approval on the idea that Europeans and Americans have formed racist cults to kill Africans and worship the deviant demon 'Ebola-Chan' (Kaufman, 2014; Kharel, 2014). The lesbian characteristics appear to be used as part of the 'grotesque/ deviant' angle in the conspiracy, given extensive homophobic violence and criminalisation of homosexuality in Nigeria during 2014 (Faul, 2014). It also seems to be associated with a way to negatively construct the US and Europe, which the white waifu represents, and which were pressuring Nigeria to reduce violence against LGBTIQ+ people at the time of the meme (Onuah, 2014). A key nation known to be spreading conspiracies particularly using LGBTIQ+ memes across the region at this time, and taking a stance against US and European LGBTIQ+ rights positions, was Russia (Jarkovska, 2019; Jones, 2019; Mueller, 2019).

Figure 1: An early 2014 Ebola-Chan meme circulated on 4chan (Kharel, 2014).

Corona-Chan: Viral Asian Lesbian Seductress Waifu

Another example of a viral virus waifu is 'Corona-chan'. She is an Asian-stylised character with slightly more knowing and heavily-lidded green eyes, little black demon wings and a more artfully ironic seductive or bad-girl-attitude allure. She is usually pictured wearing two black hair buns punctuated with green Coronavirus-shaped stems and either a body-skimming red and gold-trimmed Chinese-inspired dress or Chinese flag dress, drinking Corona beers in public settings and asking viewers if she can travel with them or perform sexual acts. She was designed as a female anime representation of the Coronavirus and cited to social media applications including 4chan, DeviantArt and others in 2020. Her representation on DeviantArt in Figure 2 and similar images often suggests she is in a sexual relationship with Ebola-Chan or also an opponent of Ebola-Chan (dp6523, 2020). Her representation as luring women becomes increasingly sexual across the memes' spread whether by designers from the same organisation or other unique individuals picking up on and adding to the meme (KreativeKaiLyn, 2020). She is also was increasingly depicted in metaphoric sexual acts with the character 'Earth-Chan'—a female character with global map patterned blue and green hair—from around May (u/ig_shame23, 2020).

Figure 2: An early 2020 Corona-Chan meme circulated on DeviantArt (dp6523, 2020).

Corona-Chan often is the more sexually aggressive of the pairing with Ebola-Chan or other females pictured, and calls either to her girlfriend or her viewer 'Come mutate me and I will set you free', 'open up to me' or similarly sexual and yet sinister lines with double entendre about death and opening up of nations' borders to Chinese influence or biological warfare and control. The pitting of these viral lesbians against each-other is achieved in a way that points to several conspiracy theories: first that China both designed and unleashed the Coronavirus, second that China is attempting a global take-over in biological warfare against the West and/or the globe in general whilst appearing attractive and helpful, and third that both China and the West/Europe are threatening to other nations. It is likely that the concomitant fetishistic sexual appeal and also the portrayal of deviance/ controversiality of these lesbian pairings helps spread the memes both amongst the often LGBTIQ+ friendly social media in the West and the anti-LGBTIQ+ media within and beyond it.

The more sexual tones of other versions of Corona-Chan memes not pictured here, like much porn-based propaganda plays on a combination of graphic sexual temptation (porn, sex, sexiness) with fear of the abject (the disturbance of the virus itself and death/ skull images aside cute female faces) to penetrate and weigh heavily on viewers' minds.

Figure 3: A May 2020 Corona-Chan meme circulated on Reddit (u/ig_shame23, 2020).

Are These Waifu Memes Propaganda?

It's highly unlikely these particular viral lesbians waifus are randomly generated memes. Despite clear effort being made for these waifus to appear as created in the first instance by disparate individual social media users from unrelated contexts, for their own pleasure in digital intimacies, everything about these memes nonetheless screams 'state-sponsored influence campaign'. One can see this using an adaptation of Ross' definition of propaganda as:

1. a charged message
2. used with the intention to persuade
3. a socially significant group of people
4. on behalf of a political institution, organization, or cause (Novaes, 2018).

For both Ebola-chan and Corona-chan, the '*charge*' comes in the memes' sexual overtones and often exaggerated racial/ethnic coding. For both the '*message*' is a conspiracy theory about 'enemy states' spreading viruses. In 2014 the 'enemy state' was US/Europe (depicted as Ebola-chan), in 2020 China (depicted as Corona-chan). These 'enemy states' are represented through the lesbian waifus as spreading viruses through LGBTIQ+ people to harm people in other nations or indeed 'the world'. The use of lesbians is not because lesbians are particularly known to be victim to, or carriers of, these or other viruses… but because they are associated with the miscasting of homosexuality in general as virus-related. This conspiracy message is particularly identical to one found in historical print media disinformation studies; which outlined how Soviet-infiltrated media and academic papers promoted narratives of US government-injected gay youth as the source of HIV AIDS crises in 1980s+ (Boghardt, 2009). This Soviet campaign is commonly referred to in Western literature now as '*Operation Infektion*' (but was originally called '*Denver*'). Articles were planted by Soviets in Indian, Nigerian and (Soviet plant) German publications. Then they were re-cited 'at arms-length' by operatives in the US and 80+ countries; in 200+ periodicals in 25+ languages. More successful narratives in that campaign used real data by trusted German biology professors like Jakob Segal (Segal, Segal, & Dehmlow, 1987) and were smuggled in to trusted British newspapers (Boghardt, 2009). These days, it is much easier and more effective for propagandists to skip the process of penetrating academia and press, by directly penetrating social groups online including via Facebook, Reddit, Instagram, Twitter and so forth. Closed and tribalized online communities such as waifu worship communities have a high trust of perceived community members and distrust of openly declared outsiders or officials who might seek to expose their messaging and identities. This makes them especially vulnerable to being targeted for propaganda in cyberwarfare efforts by foreign governments posing as 'one of them'; more likely to believe conspiracies shared by members, and more likely to share and spread them (Botsman, 2017; Jones, 2019; Kello, 2018).

The *socially significant groups of people* targeted for persuasion in Ebola-chan and Corona-chan memes include both progressive LGBTIQ+ people and those who find lesbian waifus outright sexually exciting (e.g. plenty of heterosexual males) and people offended by racism in the memes, *and* those conservatives repulsed by LGBTIQ+ people and people of other races and thus similarly likely to be intensely distracted and excited by them (Adams, Wright, & Lohr, 1996). These two socially significant groups are exactly the same two groups I and others have discovered to be targeted in Russian state-sponsored online meme campaigns over and over again (Boghardt, 2009; Jones, 2019; Mueller, 2019). Boghardt argued that the *Operation Infektion* campaign— effectively an AIDS-chan equivalent in audiences and messaging to Ebola-chan—was designed to scapegoat the US government especially, and to diminish its alliances. The over 3,500+ Russian Internet Research Agency (IRA) memes I have studied had functions (*the intention to persuade)* in deepening social divisions inside states such as the US or countries across Europe that Russia considered threatening, and in deepening suspicion of those states internationally, by provoking both progressive and conservative groups over LGBTI and ethnicity themes (Jones, 2019). Structures surrounding the texts (e.g. group pages such as 'LGBT United' during the US election, or now the Corona-chan Reddit board) prime social apparatuses as conduits for further influence and tactics over years (Jones, 2019).

The waifu apparatus would be even more effective for propaganda spreading than most online groups. This is especially due to the way that lovers of waifus more than other online users appear to rely on their digital intimacies with both the memes and the meme-sharing communities, and obsessively share and disseminate images of their waifu increasingly over time (Bailey & Harvey, 2019). I want to note here the use of 'chan' at the end of various lesbian waifu examples' names. In Japanese, words can be appended to names and occupation titles to convey the degree of intimacy and respect between oneself and the named party; it is impolite to misapply for example 'San' (a title of respect), 'kun' (for equals or inferiors), or 'chan' (for very familiar kin or children). Therefore a high degree of presumed intimacy is indicated by the appending of '-chan' to the name, but doubly an ambiguity about a potential child-like status contrasts disturbingly with the sexualised nature of the character used to attract viewers. Particularly, a lesbian waifu character would be more useful than a heterosexual waifu character here in attracting viewers, as lesbian sexual representations can be enjoyed by both heterosexual and homophobic men (Adams et al., 1996) and heterosexual and queer women (Snowden, Curl, Jobbins, Lavington, & Gray, 2016; Snowden & Gray, 2013). It seems clear that there is some *'intention to persuade'* at now harming China's (current dominance in) geopolitical standing in the most recent Corona-chan meme campaign. The value of this would be around keeping its dominance on global economies, incursions on certain nearby territories and powerful international political bodies in check.

We Need a Homotransnationalist Analytic

Multiple state-sponsored agencies now use transnational LGBTIQ+ propaganda memes on social media in foreign disinformation campaigns perhaps more than ever. These have been pitched at a range of applications; however they were always loosely aimed towards some over-arching shift in geopolitical power orders. Complicating the topic, states can combine *both* 'targets' *and* 'authors' of covert LGBTI education propaganda memes. So US-authored anti-LGBTI education propaganda featured in African states' rulings (Jones, 2017) and the US itself has been a target of multiple attacks—most especially here I note the massive campaigns by the Soviets and Russia (Boghardt, 2009; Jones, 2019; Mueller, 2019). State-sponsored LGBTI education propaganda memes on Chinese-run media in Australia and New Zealand give this topic local relevance (Brady, 2017; Cannane & Hui, 2019). There is a lack of studies identifying the scope, strategies and impacts of covert state-sponsored transnational LGBTI propaganda memes. There is also a lack of studies on what shields could work against them. This reflects the siloed nature of key knowledges: 'Gender, Sexuality and Education'; 'Media Studies'; 'Disinformation Studies'; 'International Relations' and 'Cybersecurity' rarely address each-other. Despite the media's, and some cyber theorists', *assumptions* of such propaganda memes' impacts on matters like Trumps election for example (Kello, 2018), in reality their impacts are unmeasured. Such propaganda memes may or may not have 'actual impacts' on sentiments on LGBTI and racial issues ... though with the increases in homophobia and racism during periods of their use it is hard not to start jumping to conclusion.

A 'homonationalism' analytic frames LGBTI discourses as having potential collusions with security-driven colonising geopolitics. Particularly, there are collusions in their creations of 'protected' queer subject positions in *national* state policies/programs *relying on* other unprotected or threatening positions nationally (Jones, 2017, 2018; Puar, 2013; Weber, 2016). In the current climate, a 'homotransnationalism' analytic is needed for studying such problems at the transnational level. It should consider LGBTI discourses as having potential collusions with security-driven colonising geopolitics in their creations of 'protected' queer subject positions in *transnational* policies/programs. Again, the focus should be on how these *rely on* or *create* other unprotected or threatening positions. This is not to say that LGBTI people create the subject positions or the memes and waifus. They may not even be their primary or only audience, or target. However, the subject positions themselves collude with geopolitics and this needs much deeper exploration.

What's the solution?

A homotransnationalist analytic is particularly useful for thinking about how the state-sponsored cyberwar campaigns that use LGBTIQ+ (and other) identities and depictions have little concern for the potential damage done to LGBTIQ+ people and people of particular racial/ ethnic profiles, in seeking to further the power of one state and diminish that of another. Sometimes transnational propaganda campaigns even have the direct intent of creating divisive climates for LGBTIQ+ people as a step towards the greater goal of division amongst perceived enemies, or have the direct goal of sexualising LGBTIQ+ people in exploitative ways… Corona-chan is simply more likely to spread effectively as a 'lesbian' and to impact people more deeply with her message, for being positioned as sexually aberrant or at the very least a sexual resource that is difficult and thus desirable to obtain. Therefore, any impacts on lesbians that come from these waifus are probably seen as just a side effect, or even a 'useable' social phenomena, for state-sponsored campaigns in the global game of thrones. Lesbian waifu identities are thus being positioned as a kind of chess-piece or weapon.

Disinformation theorists Nimmo, Laity and Herzog proposed 'information defence' and 'strategic-communication' (strat-com) to counter the division and dismay caused by state-sponsored propaganda in general (Herzog, 2011; Jackson, 2015). This pre-emptive approach targets specific '***sensitive areas***'; halting propaganda by identification and ***proper information***; and involving governments sponsoring exchanges between journalists, academics, and experts in those sensitive areas via an international network with a strong broader narrative in place to debunk it faster. Nimmo favours use of *targeted communities' experts* disseminating this information; not governments, who should be 'hands-off' to avoid perceptions of anti-propaganda messaging as being domestic propaganda (Jackson, 2015).

Conclusion

LGBTI, waifu worshippers and other digital community members need to understand that their identities *are seen as useful in propaganda*. Further, digital communities need to understand *that LGBTI issues are often targeted and LGBTI characters often used* in transnational propaganda campaigns … including current propaganda around the COVID-19 and other themes. The perceived positive and negative aspects of lesbianism have both been weaponized for artistic consumption in the memes to create feelings of deep sexual closeness and deep sexual revulsion in these waifus so that their geopolitical messages are spread internationally. However through these waifus' spread as memes, lesbianism is also suborned to more a set of tropes than to any lesbian's unique or owned experience; their weaponization is only effective to the extent the waifus are viralised. Indeed, the waifus' spread relies on lesbianism as a currency to co-opt straight male manga fans into the spread of propaganda. In particular then, lesbian and other community members need to understand the homophobic and racist misuses of certain lesbian waifus online and avoid being implicated in their adoption and spread, through misplaced intimacies.

At the very least, it is simple enough to see the logic that sharing Corona-chan memes *uncritically*, is promoting depictions of lesbians and Chinese people as dangerous killers (in the simplest view of them). Some extra effort in seeking out lesbian-produced art and forums, with real-world presences that can be verified and straight-forward ethics in representation of women, may be worthwhile when sourcing characters and imagery into the future. It would also be important to see the development of a simple broader narrative to combat LGBTI propaganda meme narratives. Networks of academics and cybersecurity experts could be used to supply research-based anti-propaganda narratives and awareness raising resources to LGBTI communities pre-empting and responding to lesbian waifu propaganda. Such networks could also serve as hubs for LGBTI community reporting of suspicious content online. Lastly, I note that social scapegoating around viruses is as old as viruses themselves; and a likely future staple in cyberwar.

References

Adams, H., Wright, L., & Lohr, B. (1996). Is Homophobia Associated With Homosexual Arousal? *Journal of Abnormal Psychology, 105*(3), 440-445.

Bailey, J., & Harvey, B. (2019). 'That pony is real sexy': My Little Pony fans, sexual abjection, and the politics of masculinity online. *Sexualities, 22*(3), 325-342.

Boghardt, T. (2009). Operation INFEKTION. *Studies in Intelligence, 53*(4), 1-24.

Botsman, R. (2017). *Who Can You Trust?* Sydney: Portfolio Penguin.

Brady, A.-M. (2017). *Magic Weapons: China's political influence activities under Xi Jinping.* Washington: Wilson Centre.

Cannane, S., & Hui, E. (2019). Federal election 2019: Anti-Labor scare campaign targets Chinese-Australians. *ABC Investigations.* Retrieved from https://www.abc.net.au/news/2019-05-03/federal-election-scare-campaign-targets-chinese-australians/11073514

dp6523. (2020). Corona-chan x Ebola-chan. Retrieved from https://knowyourmeme.com/photos/1720432-corona-chan

Faul, M. (2014). Nigeria gay arrests: Dozens arrested, and 'we are on the hunt for others'. *CSMonitor World News.* Retrieved from http://m.csmonitor.com/World/Latest-News-Wires/2014/0114/Nigeria-gay-arrests-Dozens-arrested-and-we-are-on-the-hunt-for-others

Herzog, S. (2011). Strategic Security in the Cyber Age. *Journal of Strategic Security, 4*(2), 49-60.

Jackson, L. (2015). The Three Warfares—China's New Way of War. In P. Pomerantsev (Ed.), *Information at War: From China's Three Warfares to NATO's Narratives* (pp. 5-15). London: Legatum Institute.

Jarkovska, L. (2019). The European Union as a child molester: sex education on pro-Russian websites. *Sex Education.* Retrieved from https://www.tandfonline.com/doi/full/10.1080/14681811.2019.1634041

Jones, T. (2017). Trump, Trans Students and Trans-national education polity. *Sex Education, 18*(4), 1-16. Retrieved from https://doi.org/10.1080/14681811.2017.1409620

Jones, T. (2018). South African Contributions to LGBTI Education Issues. *Sex Education, 19*(4), 455-471. Retrieved from https://doi.org/10.1080/14681811.2018.1535969

Jones, T. (2019). Double-use of LGBT youth in propaganda. *LGBT Youth,* 1-24. doi:10.1080/19361653.2019.1670121

Kaufman, S. (2014). 4chan Users Are Trying to Spread Ebola Lies in West Africa. *vocativ.* Retrieved from https://www.vocativ.com/world/nigeria-world/ebola-4chan-anime/

Kello, L. (2018). *The Virtual Weapon and International Order.* New Haven and London: Yale.

Kendall, L. (2002). *Hanging Out in the Virtual Pub: Masculinities and Relationships Online.* Oakland:: University of California Press.

Kharel, G. C. (2014). Ebola is CIA-Created Demon? Conspiracy Theory Goes Viral as Meme Shows Disease Created by 'White People'. *International Business Times.* Retrieved from https://www.ibtimes.co.in/ebola-cia-created-demon-conspiracy-theory-goes-viral-meme-shows-disease-created-by-white-people-609490

KreativeKaiLyn. (2020). Corona Chan. *DeviantArt.* Retrieved from https://www.deviantart.com/kreativekailyn/art/Corona-Chan-834123485

Mueller, R. S. (2019). *Report on the Investigation into Russian Interference in the 2016 Presidential Election.* Retrieved from Washington:

Novaes, C. D. (2018). Pornography, ideology, and propaganda: Cutting both ways. *European Journal of Philosophy, 26*(1), 1417-1426.

Onuah, F. (2014). Nigeria criminalises same-sex relationships. *The Sydney Morning Herald.* Retrieved from http://www.smh.com.au/world/-30raz.html

Puar, J. (2013). Homonationalism As Assemblage. *Jindal Global Law Review, 4*(2), 23-43.

Rubin, G. (2013). Thinking sex: Notes for a radical theory of the politics of sexuality. In P. Nardi & B. Schneider (Eds.), *Social Perspectives in Lesbian and Gay Studies.* New York: Routledge.

Segal, J., Segal, L., & Dehmlow, R. (1987). *AIDS: its nature and origin.* Nundah: Bertrand Russell Peace Foundation Australian Branch.

Snowden, R., Curl, C., Jobbins, K., Lavington, C., & Gray, N. (2016). Automatic Direction of Spatial Attention to Male Versus Female Stimuli: A Comparison of Heterosexual Men and Women. *Archives of Sexual Behavior, 45*(4), 843-853.

Snowden, R., & Gray, N. (2013). Implicit Sexual Associations in Heterosexual and Homosexual Women and Men. *Archives of Sexual Behavior, 42*(1), 475-485.

u/ig_shame23. (2020). Corona-chan yuri. *Reddit.* Retrieved from https://www.reddit.com/r/coronachan/comments/gnyw7j/coronachan_yuri/

Weber, C. (2016). *Queer International Relations.* New York: OUP.

Tiffany Jones is an Associate Professor in the Department of Educational Studies, Macquarie University. She researches LGBTIQ+ issues in education, education policy, health and social policy, and election security. She is the series editor-in-chief of *Bent Street*.

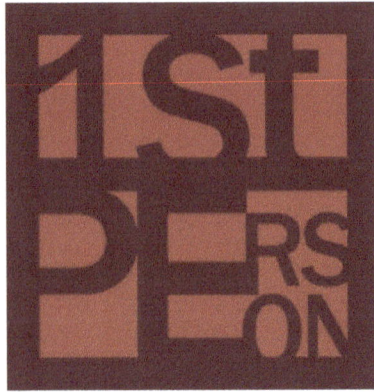

NOT SO DISTANT
DENNIS ALTMAN

Community politics, social distancing and pandemics old and new

On March 27 Juan Carlos sent me a video taken from his balcony, of police and military enforcing a curfew in Quito. This was not the first time Ecuador has been under curfew: six months ago the government imposed curfews in reaction to mass protests, led by indigenous groups, against austerity measures imposed by the government of President Lenin [sic] Moreno.

Had the pandemic not happened we would have been together at a conference in Honolulu, marking two years since we first met at a similar conference in San Francisco in 2018. We've stayed close ever since, and have spent perhaps seventeen weeks together, in the United States, in Melbourne and, most romantically, on a cruise up the coast of Norway. For the first time since we met there can be no plans to see each other again.

Global lockdowns have disrupted relationships in all sorts of ways, either forcing people apart or ironically forcing them too much together. There will almost certainly be a slew of coronavirus divorces, pregnancies, break-ups and new romances. Marilyn Monroe allegedly said, 'it's better to be unhappy alone than to be unhappy with someone else' and the pandemic has tested this in unpredictable ways.

For Juan Carlos, who teaches at a University in Ecuador, the pandemic has meant enforced isolation and a massive workload as he struggles with an inadequate laptop and students who don't always have good internet access. I'm semi-retired and work from home: 'So what', Juan Carlos asks, 'is different for you?'

The lockdown he faces is far more draconian than ours; currently there is a curfew that extends from 2.00pm to 6.00 am and outdoor exercise is forbidden. He has had no social contact for three weeks; on the one day he can drive he takes food to his mother but leaves it outside her door.

The pandemic in Ecuador was one of the first in Latin America, with scary images coming from the port city of Guayaquil of people being turned away from hospitals, of bodies lying in homes because they cannot be collected for burial. By the beginning of May 1700 people had died in Ecuador, which has a population smaller than Australia's, and the pandemic was threatening a number of indigenous communities. Now similar stories are emerging from Mexico, Pakistan, Iraq.

*

We have been here before. For gay men of the generation who experienced the worst ravages of the AIDS pandemic there are unsettling parallels in our experience of coronavirus. The demands for social isolation remind many of us of the panic in the early days of the AIDS pandemic when there were irrational fears that any contact with a suspected 'carrier' could lead to infection: men were refused treatment, hospital patients had food thrust under doors by nervous orderlies, there were demands for quarantine and the closure of sex venues.

COVID-19 is far more easily transmitted; has a lower death rate than AIDS before the development of ARV therapy, though deaths came in general more slowly, as HIV destroyed the immune system and laid bodies open to a myriad of infections. Most important Covid is not associated with stigmatised behaviors around sex and drugs, although it has produced its own share of stigma. As with AIDS COVID-19 has produced a search for culprits: in Guayaquil, one woman, who'd arrived on a plane from Spain at the onset of the pandemic, was targeted as the source of the city's pandemic. In Australia we have seen attacks on people of Chinese descent; it is only a few months ago, in the early innocent days of the pandemic, that we were encouraging people to eat at Chinese restaurants to counter racist attacks. The President of the United States has been determined to blame China for the pandemic, shifting attention away from his deliberate reduction of the country's ability to respond to new pandemic diseases.

Once HIV was identified as the cause of AIDS it also became clear that the retrovirus could only be transmitted through what was coyly termed 'exchange of bodily fluids', so that semen and blood were identified as the routes of infection. The greatest death toll in those early years was among young men with haemophilia, who had received infected blood products, but preventing the transmission of HIV required far less caution than does coronavirus. Now we are told to avoid any close contact in ways that disrupt vast swathes of what we had taken for granted as part of everyday life.

We in Australia have been spared the grim death toll that's affected so much else of the world. The pages of death notices that appeared in the gay press before effective therapies were developed against HIV have no counterpart in Australia to date, but they are matched in New York, Milan, Sao Paulo.

What is common to living through the two pandemics is the sense of anxiety, the fear that even when we take all reasonable precautions the virus might sneak up on us unexpectedly. One friend who is objectively at low risk managed to get tested three times before the end of April, recalling those gay men who during the early years of AIDS would seek out tests even when they had not put themselves at risk of exposure. And as with HIV tests it is possible to get tested negative on Wednesday, be infected on Thursday and pass on the virus, unnecessarily confident in one's status.

Three months into the pandemic I am interviewed on zoom by Steven Dansky, whom I knew in the early halcyon days of gay liberation in New York. He wants to find a queer angle to the pandemic, but I struggle: unlike AIDS the impact of COVID-19 is greater according to age and class but not, I think, to sexuality. The restrictions on movement are hard on people not in live-in relationships, even more so on those in toxic living situations, whether with partners or housemates. For people used to finding intimacy through bars or on-line hook-ups there is a sudden hole in their lives, and this may be truer for more gay men than heterosexuals, but not for those in monogamous relationships. 'Think of the trans* sex-workers who've lost their income' says Steve, but isolation has been tough on all sex workers, as it has on most people who supply personal services.

*

As with COVID-19 Australia's response to AIDS was generally regarded as one of the best globally. In both cases there was considerable bipartisanship, in contrast to the United States under either Reagan or Trump. With the support of Prime Minister Hawke, the Health Minister Neal Blewett was able to develop a national program of HIV prevention which kept cases to a far lower level than in the United States. The states were less unified than they have been around COVID-19; Queensland under Bjelke-Petersen was particularly recalcitrant, so that money for the Queensland AIDS Council was funnelled through an order of Catholic nuns. But key figures in the Liberal party ensured the federal response was maintained.

Some of the leaders from the HIV world have emerged as leading authorities in the coronavirus response. Tony Fauci, the most trusted medical authority in the United States, was a key figure in developing anit-retrovirals to treat HIV and the White House coordinator of the COVID response (1), Deborah Birx, has overseen the AIDS response for both Presidents Obama and Trump. In Australia there has been key input from people like Bill Bowtell, who was the chief advisor to Health Minister Blewett at the outbreak of the pandemic, Sharon Lewin from the Doherty Institute who is leading research into a possible HIV cure and Michael Kidd, now Principal Medical Advisor to the federal government, who chaired one of the federal government's advisory committees on HIV.

But that is where the parallels end. If there are fears that Australia is too prone to follow American models our response to COVID-19 suggests that there are distinct differences in our political cultures which a crisis highlights. It is obvious that the Australian response to the pandemic has been far more united and successful than that in the United States, both in terms of public health and economic support. The pandemic has, yet again, revealed the extraordinary shortcomings of the United States health system.

As in the case of AIDS, the United States, with its complex patchwork of federal, state and local authorities, was far slower to develop effective prevention. This was most marked in the case of needle users; while Australia prevented a major outbreak through the early institution of needle exchanges, these became hostage to the Reagan Administration's war on drugs and are still not available across the country.

In the current pandemic the cultural differences between the two countries are most evident is in angry widespread demonstrations against lockdowns across the United States. Trust in government has remained sufficiently robust in Australia for the great majority to accept lockdowns. [Research from the US Studies Centre suggests far greater acceptance of government restrictions in Australia than the United States.] While there have been grumbles from occasional commentators there has been largescale acceptance of extraordinary measures taken in the name of public health.

Yes, there has been a least one demonstration outside the Victorian Parliament house on Sunday May 10, spurred by a ratbag collection of conspiracy theorists including anti-vaxxers, climate change sceptics and one woman who claimed Microsoft founder Bill Gates was orchestrating the pandemic (2). But we have not experienced the virulence of political debate in the United States where Dr Fauci has become the target for extreme hate mail and many Trump supporters view the pandemic as a plot aimed at the President. It's significant that our response has been led by a conservative Prime Minister who has consistently deferred to health expertise rather than right wing commentators.

Any major pandemic will accentuate existing inequalities. This is apparent in the United States where, as with HIV, there is a larger impact on non-white and poor populations, related to existing poor health conditions and lack of access to medical care (3). Here the failure of the government to extend any form of income protection to perhaps a million casual workers and international students is causing widespread misery.

COVID-19 has received so much attention because unlike, say, the Ebola outbreak earlier this decade, it quickly affected rich countries. Globally the pandemic is probably still in its early stages. But social isolation and good hygiene is far more difficult in low-income countries where people live in cramped conditions, often without safe water supplies. When India suddenly imposed rigid shutdown measures it created conditions of extreme hardship for millions of people dependent on casual work and without proper housing. UN Agencies are warning of catastrophic possibilities if the pandemic takes hold in major refugee camps.

As with COVID-19 the World Health Organisation came under fire for its slow response to AIDS, leading to the establishment of a specific agent, UNAIDS in 1994 to coordinate global responses. The combination of pressure from community organisations, and the leadership of Bush, Blair and Chirac meant a remarkable array of global resources, and the establishment in 2002 of the Global Fund to fight AIDS, Tuberculosis and Malaria. Sadly the bitter name calling between the United States and China makes international cooperation more difficult in face of COVID-19.

A couple of weeks after Ecuador went into lockdown I suggest to Juan Carlos that we write something together about the pandemic in Ecuador, which I expect will be easy to get published in Australia. I am taken aback when one editor tells me there's no interest in Latin America, but should I be surprised?

The need to control the pandemic has forced a closure of borders in ways that two months ago could only have been a wet dream for the most committed isolationist. Not only is international travel almost totally abandoned, even travel between states is now heavily policed. Where once we fantasised about visiting Venice or Borobudur, now a trip to Surfers is forbidden.

My fear is that necessary physical isolation will encourage a growing chauvinism and rejection of the outside world in favour of a narrow Australian chauvinism. Certainly the impact on travel will be felt for years: who would now feel confident embarking on a cruise? Which foreign student will want to come to study in a country that has made clear they are the first to be abandoned when things get tough?

Ours is a melancholic, not a sad separation. It does not compare with the awful enforced separations that infection, war, expatriation, incarceration forces on millions of people, separations that will only be intensified by corona-inspired lockdowns. After all, as a wise friend pointed out, ours has been a virtual relationship for most of the past two years. The difference now is that there is no fixed point where the virtual might become real. The pandemic has upset our very notion of the future.

On Fauci see Michael Specter: 'The Good Doctor' *New Yorker* 20 April 2020.
[2] 'Ten arrested, officer injured at rally' *The Age* 11 May 2020.
[3] James Hargreaves and Calum Davey: 'Three lessons for the COVID-19 response from pandemic HIV' published April 13, 2020: https://doi.org/10.1016/S2352-3018(20)30110-7.

Dennis Altman AM FASSA is Professorial Fellow in Human Security at La Trobe University, and the author of many books, including the recent *Unrequited Love: Diary of an Accidental Activist* (Monash Publishing, 2019). This article first appeared on the *Meanjin* blog on 13 May 2020.

BODY IN RETROGRADE
SAMUEL LUKE BEATTY

Body in Retrograde is an intimate collection of comics that illustrate some of the complications Samuel experienced while healing from his top surgery. The work is centred in outer space, yet grounded in the reality of having a body in recovery. The comics use cosmic themes to address unexpected imperfections about his surgery results; focusing on the scar formation, open wounds and concave tissue in the chest. He relates these bodily experiences to planetary bodies, blackholes, impact craters, retrograde orbits, and even supernovae.

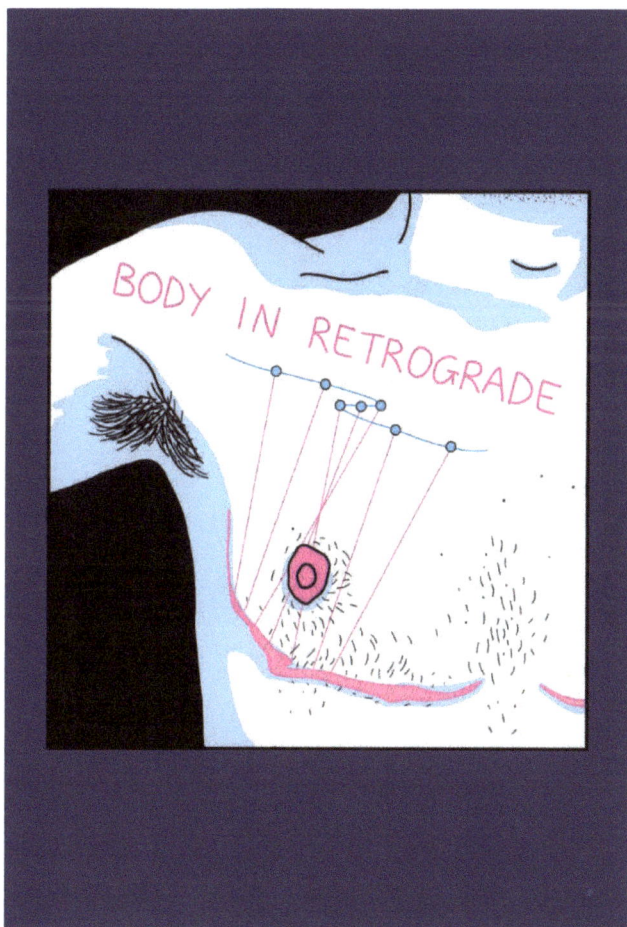

THESE SCARS
STRING ACROSS
MY CHEST

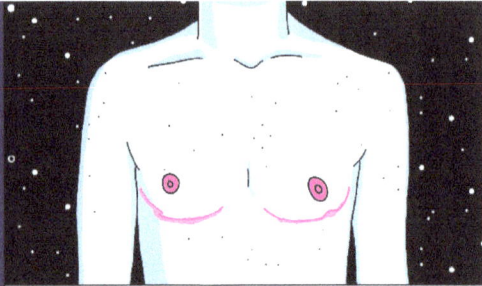

LIKE CONSTELLATIONS OF STARS.

OBSERVED

TOP SURGERY: WEEKS

RECORDED

AND CHARTED.

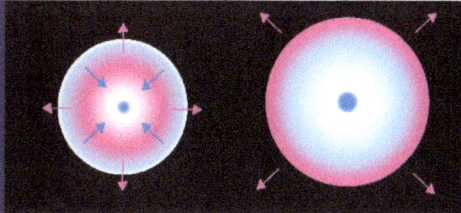

SOME STARS UNDERGO GRAVITATIONAL COLLAPSE.

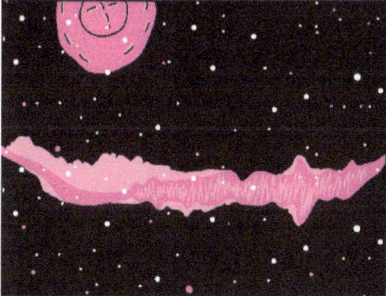

THEY RADIATE ENERGY,

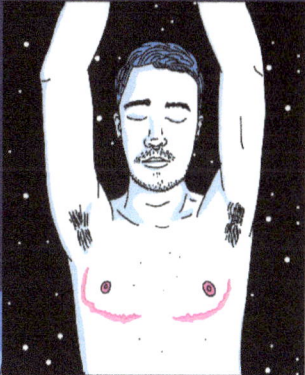

LUMINOUS FORMS,

EXPANDING INTO SUPERNOVAE.

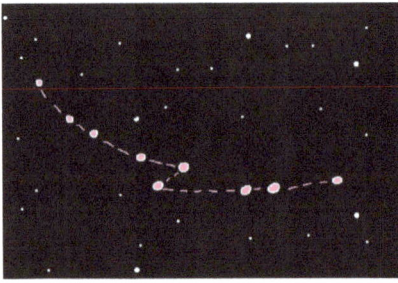

SOME STARS FADE OVER TIME,

OTHERS COLLAPSE INTO BLACK HOLES.

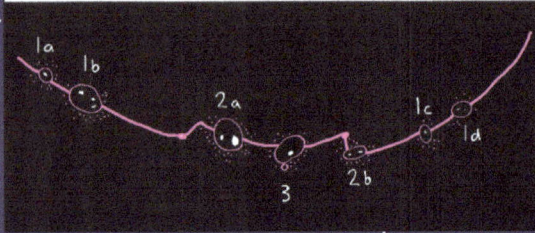

UNSTABLE,

INVISIBLE BODIES

COMPACT STARS		
1 a-b		07/11/18
1c		12/11/18
1d		12/11/18
2a		21/12/18
2b		22/12/18
3		26/12/18

FROM INTERNAL PRESSURE.

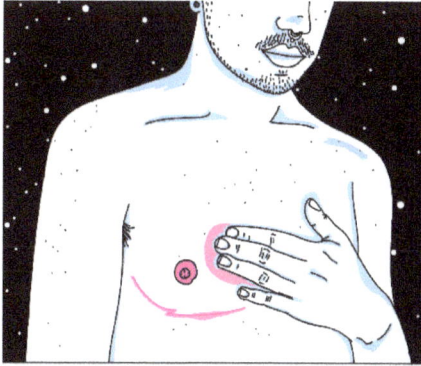

THERE'S A CRATER IN MY CHEST.

IT DIPS CLOSE TO THE BONE.

A CONCAVE IMPACT,

COLLIDING WITH

MY PLANETARY BODY.

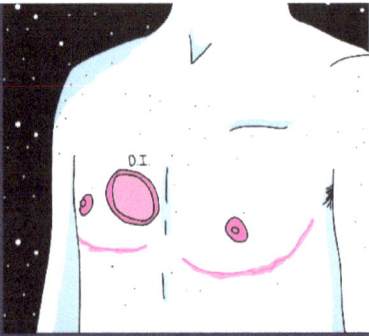

FROM REMOVAL

AND RECONSTRUCTION.

IN THIS

POST- OPERATIVE

ATMOSPHERE.

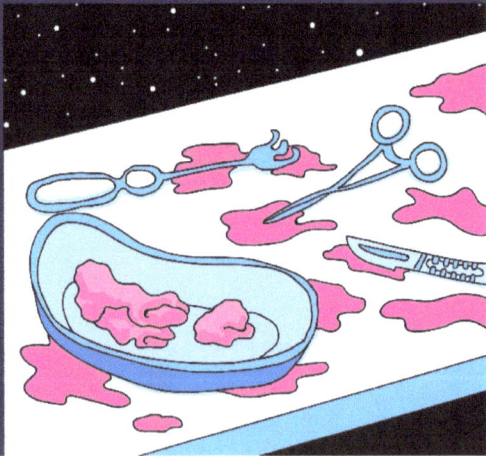

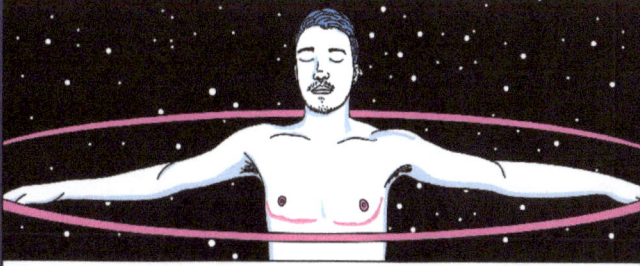

I AM A PLANETARY BODY IN CONTINUOUS ORBIT.

AN ENTIRE CORE FORMED IN TRANSITION.

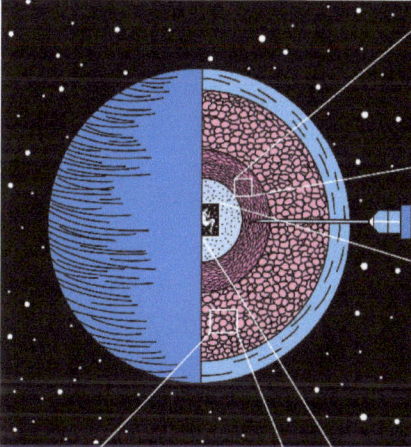

COMPOSED OF

ESSENTIAL ELEMENTS

ALLOWING ME

TO GROW.

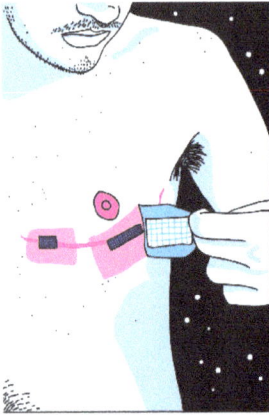

SCAR TISSUE DEGRADE.

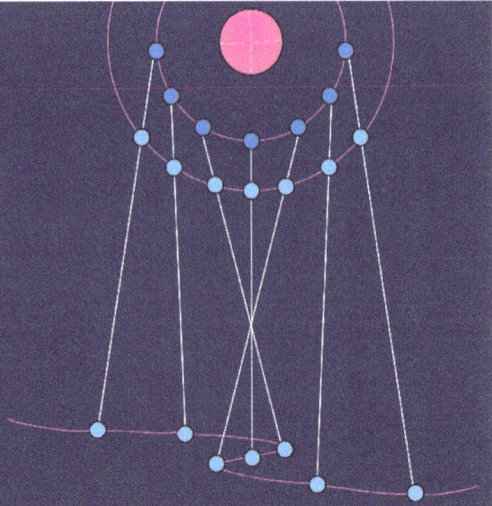

BODY IN RETROGRADE.

HEALING ISN'T LINEAR

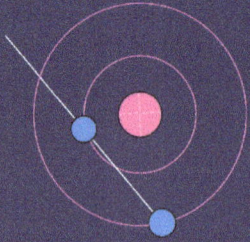

BUT I'M ON THE RIGHT PATH.

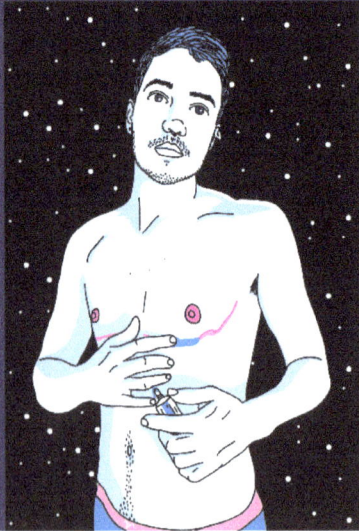

These comics were exhibited as part of 'Body In Retrograde', Samuel's first solo show, at Goodspace Gallery on 22 January 2020

Samuel Luke Beatty works with traditional and digital illustration, as well as forms of printmaking and bookbinding zines and artist books. His practice currently uses storytelling and the metaphor of space exploration across graphic narratives to discuss complexities of gender identity in relation to his own experiences as a transgender man. Samuel lives and works in Sydney, Australia.
www.samuellukeart.com

ARCHITECTURE AT NIGHT
MICHELLE DICINOSKI

Several years back, over a period of a week, I started to hear my father's voice just as I was falling asleep. He was calling my name as though he were standing nearby.

'Michelle,' he'd say. 'Michelle.'

It was weird. He lived a day's drive away from me then, so it made no sense to hear this voice. I would wake up with a start and look around the room, thinking my father must somehow be there with me. But it was always a dream.

After the first few times it happened, I trained myself to follow the voice into the dream, instead of back into the waking world. To realise I was being called forward, not back.

*

I've been thinking about voices a lot lately. It's partly because I've moved to a new country and my accent marks me as different here. My vowels swell in ways that people aren't used to.

'A?' people say, as I try to spell my name to them.

'I,' I say. '*I*.'

*

I read an interview with the cultural critic Masha Tupitsyn, who is also interested in voices. She says, 'If listening is about presence and resonance, it creates the kind of relational space that expands and amplifies the volume of intimacy.' Looking doesn't do this. 'The ear,' Tupitsyn says, 'is the only aperture you cannot close.'

*

But there are ways to close the ear. I think of how I used to spend hours on the phone with people I no longer speak to at all.

*

Sometimes I imagine how the conversation might start.

 WOMAN 1: Hi.

 WOMAN 2: Hi.

 WOMAN 1: So. *(Exhales softly.)* It's been a little while.

*

On the first real spring day, I walk through the Common at noon and the leaves are so green that they don't seem real. I think about you and wonder if it's warm there. A group of five men, jacketless, play on the grass with a soft bat and ball, their pink and blue ties flying as they run. It's the kind of thing I want to tell someone about. It's the kind of thing I want to tell you about—how spring has dropped at last and at once, like a curtain.

*

People don't like to talk on the phone anymore. The number one reason cited for this reluctance is that telephone calls are disruptive. We don't like surprises like this anymore—or maybe we never did. We like to control who comes into our space. We like to control when and how we respond—or if we respond at all. We like our responses to be studied, careful, appropriate, and, most of all, not too eager. We neither want to *be* disrupted, nor to *seem* disrupted.

*

WOMAN 1: I'm just putting my headphones in. Can you still hear me?

WOMAN 2: Yes, that's good. Loud and clear.

*

For a long time, you were my only friend on this new continent. Though we live far away from each other, I still liked knowing you were there. I talked to you as I went places, or didn't. As I walked by the river. As I crossed the green metal bridge. In the bath. On a train. Lying on the bed. Staring out the window at the endless snow.

*

Another reason people don't like talking on the phone is because it's one-to-one communication, instead of the one-to-many communication of social media. Why call five friends to tell them each the same news when you can tell five hundred or a thousand at once? And telephone calls can take up so much time. They're just so inefficient.

*

In literature, voice refers to something beyond spoken language. It's about the unique sound of the narrator, the sense of character that is constructed by elements like word choice, sentence length, syntax. It's also about a relational style: what the narrator chooses to tell, and how. In making these choices, the writer shapes the perceived closeness or remoteness of the narrator. That's an important thing. Intimacy and distance. How they're built. How they shift.

*

When I was a kid, we didn't *call* people; we *rang*. There's a difference. To call is to hail, to address. To call is to cry out. To call is to name. In calling you, or calling to you, I identify you. To ring is something else again. To ring is to sound like a bell. But to say the word 'ring' also makes me think of the other kind of rings. Of promises and unbroken circles. Of things that we hope will last.

*

To make sound, including speech itself, you need two things, says the voice coach Cicely Berry: that which strikes, and that which is struck and 'which resists the impact to a greater or lesser degree and vibrates accordingly.'

*

Last spring you went to a vineyard by a bay. Afterwards you called me to tell me about it. There was an old-fashioned red telephone box in the middle of the vineyard, you said. And, improbably, there was a working telephone inside. Visitors could go inside and call anyone they liked, free of charge. You were going to ring me, you said, but there was a long queue of tourists. I googled the vineyard when you told me about it, and there it was on my screen: a fire-engine red phone booth, a blue summer sky above it, and rows of green vines stretching off into the distance.

*

Like most kids, I was fascinated by telephones when I was very young. My grandmother's wall phone was a golden yellow, the color of melted butter. I still remember how it felt: smooth handset, the resistance of the rotary dial against my fingertip, the heat of my ear after a long conversation. To remember this phone is to remember not just talk, but also skin. It's been decades since I touched a phone like this, but I still feel it in my fingertips when I think of it. Where does this memory live? Will it ever go away?

*

WOMAN 1: Hello. It's me. Is this a good time?
WOMAN 2: Hi. Yes, just let me put you on speaker. Now, let me get settled.

*

In my imaginary phone calls, I can never get past the preliminaries to the part where we actually say something of consequence. This means I don't know what I want to say, or I do know, but don't want to say it. Or perhaps I'm frightened of what you might say. Perhaps I'm frightened that you won't say anything at all.

*

People seem less concerned with voice in nonfiction than in fiction. In memoir and other forms of creative nonfiction, voice is maybe seen as a given. Natural. Documentary. Like the genres themselves are assumed to be. There's a general sense that there's an ease to this form of communication. How hard can it be? You're just saying what's true, in the same way that you just open your mouth and talk.

*

There are special descriptors for different qualities of voice. Some of them are familiar words, like *breathy*, and *creaky*, and *hoarse*. But some are less familiar, verbs that emphasize the action involved in voice. Words like *bleat, fry, flutter,* and *shimmer*. Words like *pressed* and *strained*.

*

Sometimes we talked through the sunset. The light turned from yellow to gold to grey, and then the room was grainy. I could hear things in the distance: a neighbor arriving home, a snatch of music from a car radio, a door slamming, the jingle of keys outside. But they belonged to another time. There on my back on the sofa in a dark room, I was somewhere else, somewhere in between.

*

Another memory of old phones: tracing the helix of the phone cord while talking, feeling the smooth plastic that coated the taut wire, slipping a finger into the coil of the cord. There it was, disappearing. There it was, reappearing. All the while, the person on the other end of the line, the voice.

*

The writer Ian Bogost says that 'the handset made telephone calls an undeniably carnal art, one in which a foreign apparatus came into close contact with one's face, ear, and lips.' It's true. Talking on the phone wasn't just talking. It was mouth sounds: sighing, sipping, swallowing, the rearrangement of lips and tongue. Later on, when I was older and living in sharehouses and could drag the phone outside on a long cord, it was the sound of smoking, the long notes of inhalation and exhalation. It was always bodily, even while it was remote.

*

It feels like being a teenager again, this going from speaking to not speaking. I don't know what to do about it. I pretended everything was okay, and so did you, even as you slowly disappeared. By disappeared, I mean you went silent.

*

A while back I listened to a podcast where a middle-aged gay man from rural Alabama described what it was like to talk on the phone for hours with his friend, another gay man. Sometimes the sun would set and he wouldn't turn the lights on, but would just sit in the dark house, talking. *I remember that*, I thought.

Not their particular conversation, but the feel of hundreds of conversations like that. Conversations I had in my teens. Conversations I had last month. Conversations I had with you.

As the man in the podcast spoke about those phone calls, I listened to him in that immersive way I used to listen on the phone and something strange happened. Time seemed to double back on itself, loop, and catch me and this man there inside it. I don't think there's a word for this net of feeling, for all the things that knotted together to make it. I just know it was about loneliness and distance, the things we don't know how to call for, or the things we want to call for but are scared will never come. It made my chest hurt.

*

'If we sit and talk in a dark room,' Marshall McLuhan says, 'words suddenly acquire new meanings and different textures. They are richer, even more than architecture, which Le Corbusier rightly says can best be felt at night.' Maybe this is what happens. Or maybe it's not the words themselves that change, but our bodies. Perhaps at night we surrender to the impact of voices and let ourselves be struck.

*

In movies and sitcoms, the unwillingness to end a phone call has become shorthand for a childish and sentimental romance.

'You hang up,' a teenage girl on a pink telephone says.

Cut to a boy on the other end of the line, grinning.

'No, you hang up,' he says. And you know that you're meant to laugh at them, at their unwillingness to separate.

This is funny because knowing when to stop makes us anxious. In a form as meandering as the telephone call, what's an appropriate ending? In a form as meandering as a friendship, is there ever a right place to stop?

In a form as meandering as a life, what should we leave unsaid? None of us really knows.

*

Telephones remind us that sometimes distance lets us be closer to the people we love. Maybe that's why we like to speak in the dark, because it further disturbs our sense of what's near and what's far. The person speaking into your hot ear could be right there, or a world away— whichever feels necessary.

*

In the time when we finally talk, it will be dark again. We'll arrange a time by message, not wanting to disrupt each other. And there you'll be, you with your long vowels and your quietness and your insufficient explanations. Sometimes people just disappear, and there is no good reason. Sometimes they go silent for reasons we can't understand. Afterwards, writing about it, I won't know how to end the story, in the same way I didn't, for a long time, know how to start the conversation. How do we break without ending, or end without breaking? How do we know what to call for?

Michelle Dicinoski is the author of the poetry collection *Electricity for Beginners* and the memoir *Ghost Wife*. She has a PhD in creative writing from the University of Queensland and lives in Western Massachusetts.

TINY ESSENTIAL VICTORIES
GUY JAMES WHITWORTH

You know those laminated cards in the back pocket of seats on planes you always ignore? Specifically, the illustration that explains you should only help others with the oxygen masks that drop from the ceiling after you've helped yourself? Well let me tell you, them is wise fucking words those.

During the shut-down for COVID-19 I struggled. I mean, obviously we all struggled in various ways and various degrees. Jeez, tough audience, but since you are calling me out on it, sure, I probably didn't struggle the most out of everyone I know, but this privileged white child's struggle still felt real enough, nonetheless. A big part of that was everybody telling me what an awesome time this was for artists; all that time to sit indoors and create, they couldn't wait to see all the work I'd produce!

Fuck off fuckers.

The creative part of my brain doesn't really work in that way, and I, burdened by the drama of probable death, society's imminent collapse and the shortage of toilet paper, freaked myself out into an almost artistic standstill and I barely ventured into my studio. My creative urges suddenly felt very stifled under the weight of everyone's expectations. I called this COVIDcreativeblock19

All of a sudden, there was a lot of things that I really needed to watch on Netflix, Stan and Disney+.

In truth, I felt scared to peel back the seal on my thought process and my mental activity veered erratically between 'WE"RE ALL GONNA DIE' and 'what's the fuckin point? I might just stay in bed' and 'If I could paint hands better this pandemic might never have happened.'

This 'unprecedented' break down of societal structure did fall conveniently into the months just before No Meat May kicked off (an annual challenge I run with my partner Ryan—look it up, it's fun—you get to save the planet by just saying no thank you to sausage rolls!) so I kind of busied myself with that, thinking up slogans, photographing delicious plant-based food and cobbling together edgy left-of-centre graphics for the campaign. However, it quickly became clear my random, overly enthusiastic but haphazardly thought-through input, wasn't really appreciated by Ryan, so I kind of backed away from that too. This further compounded the 'everything I do is pointless' feeling.

I absentmindedly attempted to paint a portrait (remotely from photographs) of a friend who is a therapist, who, when I rang to offer excuses about why the portrait was taking so long, shared some wise advice with me. She said, 'Maybe the best we are able to do is to just get through this as best we can with as little self-damage as we can', and that wise advice really triggered a slow change of mindset.

I'd unwittingly taken the side of the baying crowd and was expecting too much of myself. Perform monkey, perform! Jeez, surely if anybody should know my lazy-ass-limits it's me! Once I removed (or rather just wandered off and ignored) the pressure I felt from others to create culturally relevant masterpieces on an hourly basis, and blocked out the constant bulletins of badly foreboding news so readily available on social media, I found there was still an indefinable creativity there within me waiting to cautiously peer out and allow its potential to be considered.

That was the end of one struggle and the start of the next. I've never been one to be overawed by the big, blank, white of a bare canvas. I am way too man-confident and uneducated to be intimidated by such thoughts; but I still found myself sluggish and fearful of what possibly dark paths my creative thoughts may lead me down. As is often the case with depression and mental health issues, I found it all just a bit too difficult to get started; every task was too demanding. I had the tools. I had the time. I had the technical abilities, but I could not convince myself there was any worth to it.

So, I started giving myself tiny, fun creative assignments to complete. Scale was the key. Very small and undemanding projects which I could abandon without issue if I decided. I allowed myself more time of just sitting in my studio contemplating things. I chose to paint on objects that were not expensive canvases, but disposable and 'found' items. A few months earlier I had climbed into a skip (don't judge me, I'm an artist darling, I'm an artist!) to rescue some round wood offcuts and I started playing with those. And rather than encouraging myself to think up a large narrative to execute, I chose to let my mind just go wherever it chose in whatever scale it felt comfortable with.

Rainbows: rainbows are easy! These pieces were just small technical tests; could I paint a 50% tonal difference in rainbow range of shades without measuring out the paint? Turns out (mostly, kinda, convincingly) I could. I collectively christened a lot of these test pieces 'Tiny Essential Victories' a few of them turned out a tad rubbish, and that was okay, they still served a purpose as practice pieces.

However, even these small steps sometimes felt overwhelming and I deliberately took a few steps back creatively and rediscovered the simple joy of pen and paper doodling, sketching out small abstract designs built around *fleur de lys* (a constant motif in my work and a shape I can literally draw with my eyes closed). No colour, no shading, no intended outcome, slowly building up my confidence and enthusiasm around my work until I felt more able to tackle bigger projects.

And then, I received a call from a past work colleague at ACON asking if I would be interested in doing a 'Creativity for Wellness' seminar. I mean, I'd be interested, yeah, but was my creative confidence in a place where I could advise others?

While details of the session were being worked out, I set to work thinking about what I could talk about and what I could do/share/teach/advise during the seminar. I came up with the idea of offering the simplest, least demanding creative pastime I could think up and I chose to talk about some simple drawing and colouring in exercises. Start small was going to be my big message. I needed some simple black and white line drawings for the session, so I sat down in my studio and traced off the designs I had painted onto the wooden circles. Well, once I started, I drew and I drew and I drew and I drew and I literally could not stop drawing them. They flowed out.

I never studied art. I studied fashion and a tutor at fashion college once gave me some essential advice that I doubt I would have gotten in a pretentious art school; he said 'The magic of creativity only comes when it's ready, it's like a shit, if it's not ready, it won't come out, don't try to force it because at best you'll produce a wet fart.' I didn't offer this sage advice during the 'Creativity for Wellness' session as I can never say it out loud without giggling, but I offer it here along with the theme of that session which was: let's be as kind and gentle with ourselves as we can and see what we can then create. Think about the scale of what we expect from ourselves. Even during such times as a global pandemic, do not try to look after anybody else until you have looked after yourself.

But you know, also, regardless of what's happening in the world, take time to just appreciate your own tiny essential victories as you create them.

Guy James Whitworth has won various awards and has been finalist in many of Australia's art prizes. His first book, *Signs of a struggle*, has been recently published by Clouds of Magellan Press. guyjameswhitworth.com

DARK POMO
JEAN TAYLOR

PANdemIC in Melbourne

We are living through extraordinary times the like of which we've never seen before and hopefully never will again. The big disappointments for me who, at this time of the year very much enjoys getting to as many Midsumma Festival, International Women's Day, Melbourne Queer Film Festival and Comedy Festival events as I can manage and afford in order to stave off FOMO (Fear Of Missing Out), now find myself suffering, with every event and venue either cancelled, postponed or closed, from POMO (Pain of Missing Out).

Even though China had identified and reported a new lethal pneumonia in Wuhan on 31 December 2019 and by the end of January 2020 WHO had declared a world-wide public health emergency, in Australia it was business as usual. During the Midsumma Festival, 19 January–9 February, I went to several events including the Carnival in the Alexandra Gardens (sadly no Matrix Guild stall this year to take our turn on the roster) and three events at Hares & Hyenas bookshop: A Conversation with Writer Friends, (ultimately disappointing with only one out of five, Andrea Goldsmith, a lesbian writer), the ever-popular Rapid Fire and the Queer Zine and Art Fair where we had a table selling books published by Long Breast Press and Dyke Books. We enjoyed the music and hijinks in *The Top Secret Violin Case* with the band Vardos live in drag, and new classical music by queer composers in *Homophonic*, both at La Mama Courthouse as well as Goddess Grooves with an all-lesbian lineup of talented singers and musicians at Wesley Anne. We were there at the opening of A Sight For Sore Eyes featuring queer First Nations artists at the Blak Dot Gallery and the opening of two exhibitions, Dark Sepia and The Deaf Culture, at the Incinerator Gallery. We went to the Queer Playwriting Award Showcase to enjoy the 15 minute excerpts from four very talented playwrights at Gasworks. And as I've been doing since its inception in 1996, we went on the 25th anniversary Pride March carrying the Performing Older Women's Circus' banner and were a lesbian presence in solidarity at the Invasion Day Share the Spirit Concert with No Fixed Address under the trees in the Treasury Gardens.

By that time, WHO announced the new coronavirus disease would be called COVID-19 and it wasn't long before there were outbreaks of the disease in Korea, US, Iran and Europe, especially Italy, so much so that by 8 March, IWD, Italy was on lockdown. Even so, I went to the informative and educative Feminist Summer School at RMIT, 4–6 March, and was back doing volunteer work on the Victorian Women's Liberation and Lesbian Feminist Archives by indexing the lesbian and feminist photos housed at the University of Melbourne Archives in Brunswick. I was still seeing a film at the Nova Cinema in Carlton every Monday afternoon, including the documentaries *For Sama* and the Aboriginal *In My Blood It Runs* which were excellent, by the way; attended the book launch of *Out of the Madhouse: From Asylums to Caring Community?* by Sandy Jeffs and Margaret Leggett (Arcadia 2020); also Romaine Morton's session at the Indigenous Women's Filmmakers at RMIT with playwrights giving their insights into their processes; and the comedy drama musical *Black Ties* produced by the Ilbijerri Theatre Company and Te Rēhia Theatre Company from Aotearoa as part of the Asia TOPA season at the Arts Centre; plus the Sydney Road Street Party and the Blak Dot Market with lots of Indigenous art and crafts to buy. And then it was the free IWD events to attend: the digitised now-defunct Collingwood Women's Mural organised by the Victorian Archives Centre at the Public Record Office Victoria in North Melbourne; the excellent Wise Words—A Night of Intergenerational Story Telling by a lineup of lesbian and queer writers at H&H; a picnic at the Queen Victoria Women's Centre with Candy Bowers; and finally Moss's play set in country Victoria, *Running With Emus,* at La Mama Courthouse on 11 March, the day WHO declared the world was in the midst of a PANdemIC.

In Australia we were getting warnings to wash our hands frequently and only greet each other with elbow bumps and jazz hands but the dangers notwithstanding, we still managed to get to the launch of K'ua K'ua and Erub/Mer artist Destiny Deacon's book, *DESTINY*, at the NGV in St Kilda Road in the lead-up to *DESTINY* the exhibition at the NGV in Fed Square; attended the regular Lesbians Over 70s meeting to catch up with our ageing peers; saw three excellent lesbian films at the Melbourne Queer Film Festival, *Anne+* (Dutch) at the Nova, *T11*

Incomplete (US) at the Jam Factory and *Two of Us* (French) at the Nova, before everything more or less ground to a halt!

The Comedy Festival, 25 March–19 April, had already been cancelled by this stage, we'd already booked to see and were sad to miss Geraldine Hickey in *What a Surprise*, the female stand-ups in *Breast of the Fest*, Dazza and Kief in *Go Viral in Space With Ya Mum*, *Fuck Fabulous* with Sarah Ward at the Arts Centre, the Aboriginal line-up, Deadly Funny, at the Forum and *Bobby Macumber Is Extra*. When MQFF, 12–23 March, followed suit, my next five lesbian films: *The Sympathy Card*, *Laws of Desire*, *White Lie*, *The Archivettes* and *Bit*, were cancelled, (as announced previously on FB, I am donating the proceeds of these tickets back to the performers and organisers who are understandably devastated by these cancellations after all their hard work). Then La Mama cancelled all its shows including a few we'd booked in to see over the next few weeks: *We Too Us Too Me Too Too Too*, *Mrs Robinson: A Soap Cabaret*, *Hedda GablerGablerGabler* and *Ladies of the Bay*, as well as future shows we were looking forward to, like *Do Not Go Gentle* and *The Return* at the Malthouse Theatre and especially *Fun House* and *Sunshine Super Girl* by the Melbourne Theatre Company. It was especially disappointing when the extensive *Flesh After 50* program which included Ponch Hawkes' 500 Strong photographic exhibition of naked women over 50, I was one of those photographed, at the Abbotsford Convent, 28 March–3 May, was also cancelled. As was the Matrix Guild IWD Dance on 22 March, (Matrix was busy at Chillout in Daylesford on 8 March, the 10th anniversary of Jan Gladys' death). And perhaps worst of all a get-together of radical lesbian feminists had to be cancelled.

There were first 600, then 100 limits on gatherings, travel overseas was cancelled and Qantas grounded its fleet, interstate travel was okay till it wasn't, social distancing became a thing as did working from home, state borders were closing as were libraries, swimming pools and the Women's Circus. Destiny Deacon's art opening of *DESTINY* at the NGV was cancelled, and even the Nova Cinema, Counihan Gallery in Brunswick and all the cafes and public places closed (except for takeaway in cafes, if they chose to stay open) because finally the government announced that from Monday 23 March we were in lockdown and confined to our houses. There were only five reasons to go outside: to buy food and other essential items like medication, for work and education and to exercise. The following day all the schools in Victoria closed.

I went from thinking it was all a beat-up with panic buying and stock-piling of toilet paper the worst of it, to realising that as an old lesbian who was turning 76 in April and prone to asthma that I was likely to die, (most of the deaths in Italy were people over 80), and so I have more or less come to grips with all the closures and the cancellations so much so that staying at home with the odd small walking forays into the world for exercise seems like much the better option. According to the Internet, on 24 March there were 2,044 confirmed COVID-19 cases in Australia and eight deaths and in Victoria 411 confirmed and no deaths. And cruise ships were sailing time bombs.

I'm still meditating, still doing my writing work in the morning, as always, which includes writing small pieces for various US periodicals, working on the next Long Breast Press book, listing my old photos with names and dates, listing all of my novels, plays, poetry, non-fiction and short stories, both published and unpublished, in chronological order (an unsettling trip down memory lane), watching a couple of Nordic Noir series on SBS OnDemand and Netflix, reading Anne Summers' Memoir, *Unfettered and Alive*, answering emails, talking to friends and family on the phone, not visiting the grandchildren for my own safety is probably the hardest, cooking and hanging out with Ardy.

I'm well aware that being on the old age pension and living in my own house I'm in a very privileged position compared to those who have lost their jobs and their businesses and their stage shows and have to work from home and at the same time homeschool their children for who knows how long. But it still all feels very surreal. Four days ago we visited the family in the next suburb to celebrate my grandson's 17th birthday and now with lockdown and strict social distancing and me being over 70 and advised to stay at home I won't get to see the three grandchildren for however long this will take, a definite deprivation on top of losing everything else that made life fun and worthwhile.

And it's only Day Three.

*

In the grip of the COVID-19 PANdemIC it seemed I couldn't write anything that wasn't in some way in response to this deadly virus that was affecting the whole world with cancellations and restrictions being imposed left, right and centre. So, at the suggestion of a friend in Sydney,

I started a COVID-19 PANdemIC Diary to try and make sense of what was happening to me as an individual in response to this world-wide phenomenon that was affecting everyone in deadly and extraordinary ways beyond our control.

Friday 3 April 2020
I see by my diary for today that in the usual course of events I would have been heading to the University of Melbourne Archives to continue with the indexing of the photos in the Victorian Women's Liberation and Lesbian Feminist Archives Inc collection as I've been doing for the past couple of years. Instead I'm home finalising my travel story for the forthcoming Long Breast Press (LBP) Travel anthology by adding some pertinent details to the final Paris section and taking a phone call from my ex-Tai Chi teacher who rang to see if I'm okay and did I need anyone to do some shopping. I said thank you, but no.

Saturday 4 April
I went across to the post office this morning to buy the *Saturday Age, Good Weekend* and *Spectrum* and to get money out of the bank before I went for a walk around the block in the lightly falling rain, not enough even to put up my umbrella, to get some exercise.

PANdemIC State of Play on page 5 of *The Age* 4 April 2020: The National Total Number of Confirmed Cases: 5,330 and 28 deaths.

Monday 6 April
I'm with Greta Thunberg, we don't want hope, ('the thing with feathers'), we want a revolution, change, honesty, financial security, integrity, a moral compass, worthwhile work, family, community, secure housing, healthy food, art, relevant educational opportunities, fun, laughter, creativity, books, films, plays, the list is endless.

If the lockdown lasts for six months, as the governments is threatening, some people think that this enforced time on our own could lead to a new world order while others, like myself, think it's more than likely to lead to a totalitarian regime where our lives become even worse, especially if we have to wait till next year for a COVID-19 vaccine before we're allowed out of lockdown, by which time, as someone was saying on telly last night, there'll be more suicides, madness, anxiety, stress-related illnesses and life as we know it will definitely be over.

Wednesday 8 April

I've got a small and achievable list of things I want to do today: check and answer emails, rewrite and correct an article I want to sent to *Rain & Thunder*, add to my COVID-19 diary, do some Long Breast Press business and anything else that pops up that needs attending to. After lunch, I'll go for an half-an-hour walk around the streets of East Brunswick.

Monday 13 April

We're now going into the fourth week of Lockdown and while it all feels quite familiar now, I find myself crying at odd sentimental moments and still railing against the restrictions. For example, I was annoyed later in the day because a male and his teenage son were striding down the footpath towards me two abreast without any sign of giving way to me. I had moved to the grass verge to avoid them and when I challenged him about not walking single-file, and he answered that it was alright because they were family, I said, *but I'm not* and called him an idiot. Fortunately, I was relieved to see, most of the others I encountered were observing the correct social distancing.

I know how fortunate I am and how privileged that the old age pension supports me, that I have a very comfy roof over my head plus a verandah and a garden, that I have my own writing work that sustains me.

Tuesday 14 April

The stats for today: 42 more COVID-19 cases in Australia, and two of those in Tassie were off the *Ruby Princess*, with 62 deaths and over 6,400 infected and 3,598 recovered; whereas there are 500 deaths daily in Italy and 10,000 deaths in NY a city of 18 million people; while in Indonesia people dressed as ghosts are employed to frighten people back into their homes.

Thursday 16 April

After reading 'The Handmaiden of the Holy Man' chapter in Robin Morgan's *Parallax*, I sat for over an hour during which I realised that while I was concentrating on the fact that I was financially and personally privileged compared to others I was, in fact, not coping very well at all and was, indeed, in shutdown mode. An important revelation which, conversely, made me feel a lot better.

Sunday 19 April

Our usual quiet Sunday morning in bed followed by bacon and eggs on toast on the verandah in the warmth of a sunny midday and two games of Bananarama before we went back inside to get on with the day. The only unusual event started at 2pm for about an hour and a half of chatting and catching up with dear lesbian friends on Zoom because we'd had to cancel my 76th birthday lunch with them at their house, not something I was keen on, but did enable us to see as well as hear each other.

Monday 20 April

Dreamt this morning that I was launching a book and directing a play at the same time and I was worried that no-one knew their lines and it would be a shemozzle …

Wednesday 22 April

With all the talk of flattening the curve and perhaps some of the more stringent regulations being relaxed now that fewer people are being tested positive for COVID-19, I find I'm feeling a bit frightened all over again that I might catch the virus and die. Of course, I can just go on doing what I'm doing now and stay home anyway and I might just do that until I can be assured that what has happened in Singapore with a spike in infections when they relaxed the lockdown, doesn't happen here. Or more to the point, make me and Ardy more vulnerable.

Because I really wanted to hear and see Dr Lou Bennett's webinar, Sovereign Language Rematriation Through Song Pedagogy, I actually downloaded Zoom yesterday so I don't miss it. Talking with our lesbian friends via Zoom on Sunday helped me to get over my resistance …

Sunday 26 April

The three plus hours of *Music From the Homefront Concert* organised by Jimmie Barnes of Cold Chisel and Michael Gudinski on Channel 9 last night giving thanks and paying tribute to all the workers on the front line, the nurses, doctors, medics, ambos as well as the workers at the supermarkets and public transport who are all helping to keep us alive, fed and connected as well a honouring the Anzacs, was one of the best.

Thursday 30 April

Tragedy has struck an old people's facility, Newmarch House in Caddens Western Sydney NSW, because a nurse with a 'scratchy throat' wasn't tested for COVID-19 till it was far too late, a dozen patients mainly their 90s have since died with probably more deaths on the way. This highlights the vulnerability of old people and the absolute necessity for total lockdown of Nursing Homes and the need to test all of the staff at these facilities on a regular basis.

Saturday 2 May

Noting here that three well-known lesbian activists have died recently in the USA: Ariana Karen Manov, 6 October 1946–22 March 2020, aged 73, a long-time friend of Ardy's; Phyllis Lyon, 10 November 1924–9 April 2020, the widow of Del Martin, aged 95; and Jean Boudreaux, 1932–23 April 2020, better known as Shewolf, aged 88.

The day didn't get off to a good start when Ardy baled me up in the corridor as I was coming back from the toilet and on the way to the front room to start meditating to tell me that she'd been awake since 3am with a sore throat, coughing, a runny nose and sweats and was waiting till 9am to call the health clinics to be checked. I decided not to panic because Ardy looked quite well and didn't have a fever, it was more than likely just a cold and by the time I was fixing my brekky in the kitchen just before 9am I had made the decision that if Ardy decided to get tested at the Royal Melbourne Hospital that I wouldn't go with her.

Friday 8 May

With the full moon shining in my bedroom window from the west this morning when I got up at 5am, it's good to know some things aren't affected by COVID-19.

Saturday 9 May

Feeling like a warrior on a hunting and gathering expedition, I went out into the spitting rain, cold and dark at 6pm to pick up our takeaway order of fried fish, scallops, potato cake and calamari for me, and a burger for Ardy from Scales Fish & Chippery in Weston Street attached to the Tip Top apartment block. I did wonder, given the weather, if it might have been more sensible to drive but then I'd never have found a park in Weston Street nor any park in our restricted parking street when I got back, so never mind. It was warm and full of light in the large shop and unused cafe with us customers practising social distancing till I strode back out into the cold with my brown paper bag and along the bluestone laneways to home.

Monday 11 May
On *The Project* that night Daniel Andrews' new regulations for Victoria told us he was still taking a cautious approach which I was pleased to hear and that about the only restriction that was lifted from 11.59 pm on Tuesday night that really applied to me was the one about being allowed to have five visitors, limited to family and close friends. Which augured well for my granddaughter's 15th birthday and also for the Lesbians Over 70 meeting on Sunday 17 May.

Tuesday 12 May
According to ABC News online by Nicole Mills, *Coronavirus restrictions eased in Victoria to allow five visitors to a household and outdoor gatherings of 10 people.* So, kids can see their grandparents? According to that rule, it is now possible for children to see their grandparents. But that doesn't mean they should. Professor Sutton said it was up to individuals whether they shake hands, kiss or hug.

Saturday 16 May
First I was afraid I was going to die of COVID-19, then fearful of going into lockdown for an indefinite period and only allowed out to exercise, and now I'm afraid because with the easing of restrictions, I can visit friends and family and they can visit me. We even had a calendar talk this morning for the first time in weeks to see what we're doing in the immediate future. What next? I rather fear, with a runny nose and other symptoms I woke up with this morning, I might have a cold. Damn! …

Tuesday 19 May
Picked up my Vitamin D tablets at the chemist, 250 for $36, and ran across lesbian friends in one of the laneways on my short walk today and stopped and we chatted across the appropriate width of bluestones. I'm not sure if my lack of energy is just because I'm old or a symptom of something lurking in my body but all I can seem to manage is the couple

of hours I spend on the computer in the morning before I've completely run out of puff and have to put my feet up after lunch

Thursday 21 May
… and more rain yesterday, today and tomorrow.

Saturday 23 May
While on-line shopping is financially very successful, retail spending in stores is down, according to *The Project* last night, also 75 Target stores are closing and the rest will be turned over to K-Mart and all stores in Vic might all be open by next week. The number of COVID-19 cases has spiked suddenly in several countries, including Sweden, US and Switzerland. But the big news is that the Treasurer over-budgeted by $60 billion, in a $130 billion budget to cover the wages of 6.5 million workers, due to what he claims was the fault of 1,000 employers filling out their forms incorrectly. Not a good look whichever way you look at it. Now, of course, there's pressure to use that spare $60 billion on all those who also lost their jobs when festivals, events, and venues were closed and cancelled, leaving all the artists and performers and other odds and sods on temporary and casual employment, who were considered below the arbitrary cut-off point, out of work through no fault of their own and with no income at all apart from the dole.

Wednesday 27 May—Reconciliation Week
At some stage after I'd written it here, I posted this on Facebook: Today is the 53rd anniversary of the Referendum in 1967 when 90.7 Australians voted YES to allow the federal government to make laws with respect to Aboriginal and Torres Strait Islander people and also that these same Indigenous people could be legally counted in the Australian Census for the first time. Today is also the start of Reconciliation Week 2020 which will end on Wednesday 3 June which is Mabo Day and commemorates the successful application by Eddie Mabo 28 years ago in 1992 to overturn the lie of terra nullius and establish Native Title and traditional rights for Aborigines and Torres Strait Islanders.

Ardy and I actually started the day in the front room at 9am with *Sinister Wisdom*'s memorial to Shewolf *aka* Jean Boudreaux with several speakers giving moving and informative tributes to the lesbian who was best known for her *Shewolf's Directory of Wimmin's Lands* which ran to six editions and included all of the womyn-owned lands round the US and some overseas which connected lesbians who were travelling and lived on the land with each other.

Thursday 28 May

As Ardy was saying this morning, she is enjoying her life so much in lockdown, with a few forays out into the world for food and necessities, that she doesn't want to go back to the way things were.

The Zoom experience this morning on Treaties and Reconciliation organised by the Melbourne Law School and ANTaR (Australians for Native Title and Reconciliation) with speakers Tony McAvoy, barrister in Sydney, Elly Patira, Premier and Cabinet, lawyer, and Marcus Stewart, co-chair of the First People's Assembly of Victoria, was absolutely fantastic and gave some essential insights into what needs to happen around the Treaty process which is also tied up with reconciliation with Justice for Indigenous people being a key element in any negotiations towards self-determination, truth telling, the high numbers of Aboriginal people in person as well as the numbers of children still being removed from their families and community. In other words, it's still going to be an uphill battle to get anything in place.

I was moved to write a wee message on the chat: Congratulations and huge thank you to all the panelists for a clarifying and informative discussion, it has made my day, I have supported the need for self-determination, land rights and sovereignty for several decades now and I'm ashamed that all of these fundamental issues are still bogged down by the resistance from non-Aboriginal people, keep on being strong and thank you with gratitude for all the work you're doing

Monday 1 June

The official start of Winter and time for Melbournians to hunker down rather than getting out and about, quite a bit like lockdown, and while it was great to have such a mild and sunny day yesterday, it's also appropriate that it was raining when I got up at 6.30amish. Many more easing of restrictions in Victoria today, The only ones that apply to me are: *Up to 20 people allowed in people's homes, including primary residents; Libraries, youth centres and other community spaces to open, with no more than 20 people in a single area.* I'm now waiting for cinemas, performance venues, cafes and restaurants to open. Since last night, I see that another eased-up restriction might also apply to me: *Up to 50 people allowed at funerals, plus those running the ceremony.*

Wednesday 3 June—Mabo Day and the end of Reconciliation Week
I've decided not to read anymore of *Broken Song* by Barry Hill, far too dense and depressing, and started on the second in the Hanne Wilhelmsen series by Anne Holt, *Blessed Are Those Who Thirst*, changed the toner when it ran out halfway through printing *The Spin Newsletter* and enjoyed the bread pudding that Ardy had made, for arvo tea with yoghurt and coffee in the front room because it had become far too cold outside since I'd had lunch on the verandah. I didn't like the sound of the proposed Black Deaths Matter demo organised by Warriors of the Aboriginal Resistance in support of Black Deaths in Custody in Australia, scheduled for Saturday 6 June outside parliament house with 29,000 people registered to attend especially while social distancing is still mandatory and with untrustworthy cops in attendance.

Saturday 6 June
As we had agreed we wouldn't be going to the Aboriginal / Black Lives Matter rally today outside parliament house at 2pm but were at a bit of a loss as to what to do to show solidarity till a friend's email with an Aboriginal Lives Matter poster attached and the suggestion that we do our own mini-rally, solved the problem.

After an exhilarating hour holding up our signs, I put the following message on Facebook: Because it was far too dangerous for us two old lesbians to go into the city to join the rally organised by Warriors of the Aboriginal Resistance outside parliament house we had our own mini-rally with our Aboriginal Lives Matter signs on the corner of Lygon Street Brunswick East for an hour with many thumbs up and toots from cars, smiles and waves from the bicyclists and dings from trams passing by, all very gratifying to see so much support for Aboriginal and Torres Strait Islander people.

Monday 22 June
With the Nova Cinema open for business for the first time in weeks with several films on offer I decided I was prepared to go and see Ardy's choice of *Miss Fisher and the Crypt of Tears* at 1.20pm rather than my preferred choice of *Queen and Slim* at 3.25pm because I didn't want to be coming

home on the tram during peak hour. Ardy rang to see if we could book tickets, but it was no surprise, with the 20 limit on patron per session, that the tickets had sold out. I was relieved in a way, then sad, then okay again and settled in to doing the corrections and additions on my novel *Trios* and just lost all sense of time I was enjoying it so much.

Thursday 25 June
According to *The Project* last night, for the eighth day in a row the virus stats just keep on rising in Melbourne with 20 new cases, eight spread by community contact making 142 cases in total and an 80 year old man died, the first death in a month and it's now up to eight cases in Moreland. Not too surprisingly, the government has requested medical support from interstate and has also called in the Army, there are long queues at supermarkets and because people are stockpiling once again there are limits on the numbers of toilet paper, pasta and other essential items people are allowed to buy.

Saturday 27 June
When Ardy asked me why my upper arms needed extra massaging from her this week because they were much sorer than usual, I had to confess that I had been so excited and interesting in getting back to correcting *Trios* that I'd been overdoing it. It wasn't till yesterday that I made the connection between overdoing it with my writing and the increased numbers of COVID-19 in Moreland and the increased risk to myself, and how Victoria was now seen as an increased risk state as far as the rest of Australia was concerned. I'm doing more writing that I particularly enjoy to try and balance out the fact that I am back to feeling vulnerable all over again …

Jean Taylor is a radical lesbian feminist writer and political activist based on Wurundjeri Woiwurrung country Naarm, Melbourne. She has been actively engaged in the Women's Liberation Movement and lesbian feminist activism since the 1970s and has written many novels, plays, short stories and non-fiction on these and other subjects.

Jean's work can be found on www.dykebooks.com.

PRO-PO:
POLICING PRODUCTIVITY IN THE MIDST OF A PANDEMIC
JAKE CRUZ

time to get my life together, 2020 MEPXY markers on 120GSM paper—Jake Cruz

For last year's Clifford Chance ARCUS Pride Exhibition, I submitted three artworks about taking on the skins on growing up as an Australian Filipino gay boy. However, a year on and the outward social analytic response approach had been completely flipped on its head. Instead I'm approaching my behaviour during lockdown after my place of employment had shut.

I, for the most part, did not wallow in my not doing anything. Instead I found myself restructuring my day in a way that would include smaller productive tasks, such as doing laundry or a home workout, and being significantly productive enough to feel satisfied with how I made use of the day overall.

I went through little waves of attitudes, constantly alternating between sitting around in my underwear or wrapped in blankets all day, and pretending everything was an all in one sexy chic casual loungewear look and the neighbours and paparazzi were watching me through the windows, taking photos as I feigned ignorance. Need to take out the garbage? Do some groceries? Throw on a nice jacket and work the leeeeegs.

I could see the tabloids.

I found the frequency of wearing lipstick around the house far exceeding how seldom I used to, and I became extra appreciative of non-lipstick lipstick looks, such as the 'my noodles are too spicy' and the textured 'Chip Crumb Chap-lip' looks. Something small and colourful to get excited about.

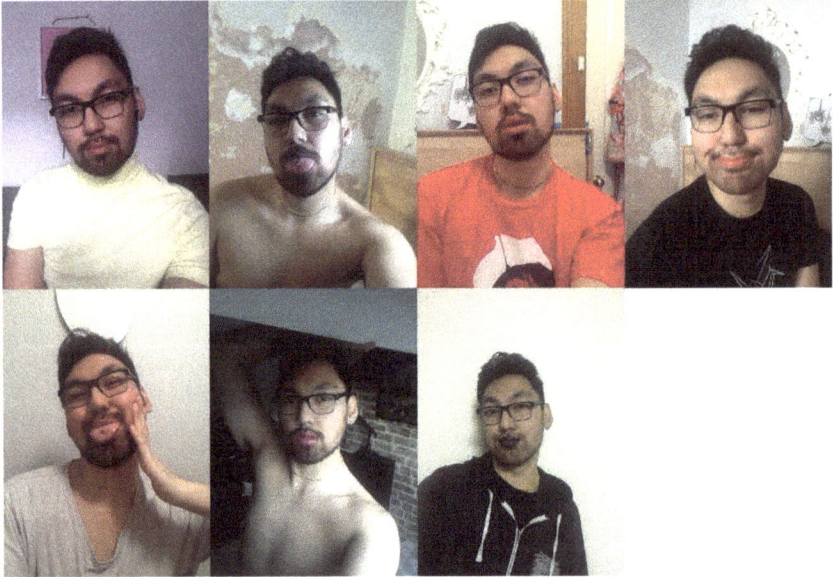

Miscellaneous lipstick documentation—Jake Cruz

Dare say I became a Cosmetic Guru over lockdown.

I spent a lot of time delving into different creative spaces through fiction or music. It felt like I was being drawn into gateways, into pockets of new places of being, where the air felt different and the gravity changed. I felt myself floating in these vacuums of the passion and commitment of the creators and I felt abundantly more creatively driven when immersed in these spaces. I felt an immense kind of intimate commonality with the feelings and mentalities of the artists towards their respective projects where they resonated with own, even if only slightly.

As a creative, the endless bounds of free time associated with lockdown seemed like a dream come true—in fact, anywhere you looked, you could see other creatives preach of project productivity, especially within online spaces. After all, I myself have so many project ideas and visions scribbled down in numerous places to pursue, and yet, this was not a sentiment I found myself sharing.

I jumped between making no artistic decisions and then beginning numerous projects, and veering off in all kinds of media, aesthetics, conceptual, and non-conceptual directions, without ever really seeing much of them through to the end. I was stuck in a creative limbo, with the freedom to do whatever I wanted and a constantly reignited drive to create; but rarely committing to a singular project for more than 3 hours or 2 days or a week. And so forth.

I began animating a simultaneously dancing and strolling figure which began as a close shot of feet walking onto the frame. This project has yet to make it beyond said shot.

I began another animation, this time of an isolated, sentient hand—also dancing—but in a simplistic manner to a beat regular enough to hypothetically allow for a freedom of song choice for accompaniment. Whilst I illustrated the key frames and orchestrated the timing, I did not illustrate the in-between frames despite the more difficult parts being completed. This project also sits unfinished at the time of writing.

Being unshowered at 2 or 3am while working away on a project was a feeling I had not known for two years, when I would regularly camp out in my university studio space for long stretches at a time. It was a feeling that became familiar once again.

At one point I decided to focus on dinosaurs and at another I filled a page illustrating an alternate design for an already existing Pokémon.

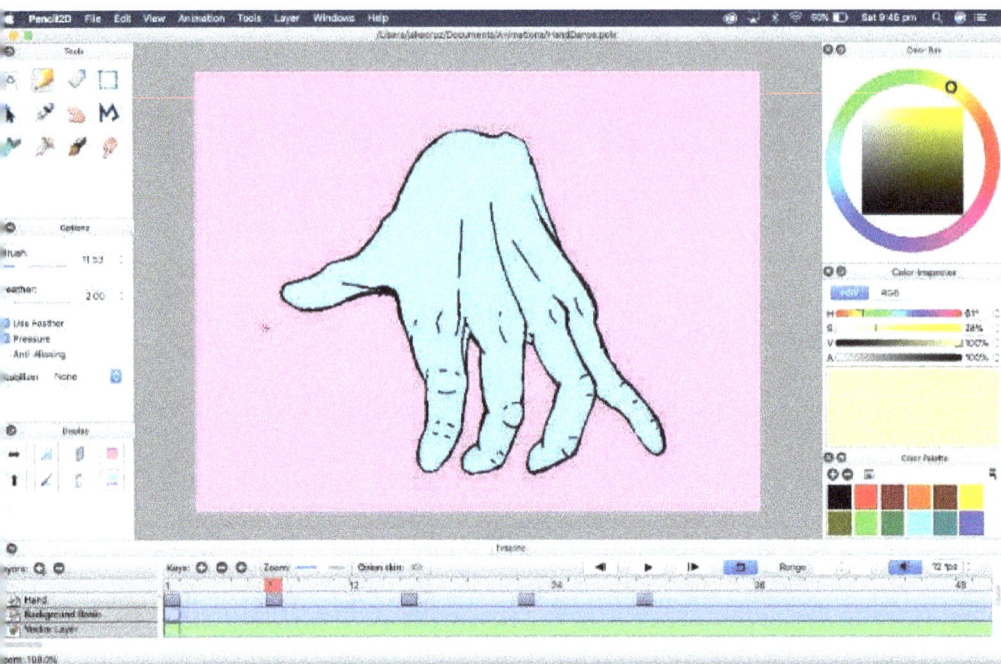

Hand dance screenshot frame #7—Jake Cruz

There were a handful of days here and there where I woke up around midday, had lunch, meandered for an hour or two, took a nap.

My laptop went with me to any room (bar the bathroom), whether I wanted to use it or not.

There were only two works I finished—the postcard design for Clifford Chance, and this piece of writing—both only due to deadlines. They help to minimise, if not erase, the embarrassment of saying 'I had an unproductive day' and for audiences to feel as though they are confiding in me. I aim to deinstitutionalise the notion of laziness for anyone beating themselves up for how they utilised their time during lockdown. It has been a time where so many are putting out such goading energies about the need for excessive productivity into the virtual world and that's an energy I don't want to contribute to as it can feel quite bulldozing.

Jake Alexander Cruz is an Australian illustrative artist who draws from his own experiences as a queer male to creates works focusing on how the body is perceived and how perceptions of his identity are read from his presentation.

LOOSE THREADS
MAX HAYWARD

I have had some practice at social isolation long before this pandemic. It was a period I call 'early adolescence'. After the blaze of glory and frantic shirt signing that was grade six graduation, my mum, brother and I moved to a new town in a waterlogged and God-fearing pocket of Gippsland. In my oversized blazer with 80s businesswoman shoulder pads, I trotted off to high school and immediately fell into the peripheral crowd that had divorced parents and loved *Lord of the Rings*.

My sort-of friends and I weren't the kind of kids that hung out on weekends or after school—it was a lunchtime and 'Is anyone sitting next to you?' kind of friendship. There were also the various people in the school cabaret production that I had secret crushes on, but apart from weeks of rehearsal, I didn't invite them around to watch *The Simpsons*. Instead I cast embarrassed glances at them across the canteen or carpark at recess. And so, for about twenty-four months, I retreated.

Not having friends is a difficult concept to grasp for some people, especially those who were good at sport in a country high school. Sport was the fabric that held much of Gippsland's youth together when I was growing up, with all the broad-shouldered, deep-voiced boys in the tightly-bound centre. The Matrix-quoters and people who spoke Elvish were somewhere on the frayed edges. I did play some sports, including soccer for four miserable months and a summer of wonky tennis, but my commitment was lacking, and I would often lose concentration half-way through a serve. To continue the fabric analogy, I was a 'loose thread'.

I noticed other loose threads out in the world beyond school grounds. They could be found buying baking supplies or quietly flicking through off-trend albums at Sanity, or discreetly reading gossip magazines at the newsagency. But mostly, my domain was domestic and centred on the family computer.

In the early 2000s, the concept of the iPhone was science fiction— Australians were still adjusting to the shock of DVDs, let alone *touch screens*—so the communal workstation was the only gateway to another digital realm. Computers weren't the family members they are now. Then, they were cautiously revered like a cabinet for grandma's silverware or china collection, placed awkwardly in a corner of the lounge or dining room, rolled out for special occasions.

Adolescent impulses and a lack of awareness around browser cookies and the concept of a 'search history' led to awkward moments for me as I became the intrepid explorer of my own sexuality. Mum would question why viruses appeared with increasing frequency, or why I'd hover around the computer if anyone else used Google or Ask Jeeves. I wrung my hands and paced around the house until I could be back on the computer searching for ways to not only erase my searches for 'big cock', but ways to stop thinking about big cock entirely.

As I attempted to supress my urge to see men doing things with each other I didn't consider even possible just months earlier, I turned to a more secluded corner of the digital world—*The Sims*, a computer game equivalent to *Big Brother* (with a substantial element of *Grand Designs*).

The Sims, for the non-loose threads, was a game in which you could recreate your own life by constructing a house and family similar to reality, or you could exaggerate everything a little (add a pool, an older sister, get a wacky haircut), or simply imagine a life where you're sharing a luxurious mansion with five topless men who are always kissing each other. It was the ultimate choose-your-own-adventure. While others trained for interschool kickboxing tournaments (or whatever it was they were doing), I was wallpapering the extension, painting landscapes in my conservatory, and hanging out in the hot tub with live-in models Chad and Andre.

Through the lens of a twenty-nine-year-old obsessed with true crime, I was clearly building a sex cult; but as a thirteen-year-old I saw this as a sexy and impeccably designed dream that filled me with less dread than porn, or actual human interaction with other year sevens.

When my school decided to effectively quarantine us from the rest of the student population in year nine, they opened up a new campus—an abandoned rope factory. Suddenly the dynamics of the year level shifted. Everyone was trapped in this weird building together with a curriculum that included paper kite aerodynamics and meditation. Sure, there were still plenty of assholes, and the more athletic kids were still popular, but there was more freedom for the frayed edges and loose threads. More freedom to occasionally reference Mordor or Galadriel, or for a boy to talk about celebrity couples. And with this breathing room came the confidence to make my first actual friends, not just theatre acquaintances, or computer-generated beings that I had designed.

During this latest social isolation, I've revisited the cultural comfort food from my childhood and adolescence, including: the highly camp favourites *The Addams Family*, *Spice World*, and *Desperate Housewives*, along with YouTube clips from Big Brother, my first forays into 'arty films' *Amelie* and *The Life Aquatic* with Steve Zissou; and a series of games where you practically play God (Rollercoaster Tycoon, Sim City 4, The Movies). And although I've been tempted to create a dreamhouse with an expert gardener hunk (me) and his astronaut husband, I have not revisited *The Sims*. Happiness seems now, more than ever, something to be lived and not just witnessed.

Max Hayward lives with his boyfriend, housemate, a library of half-read books and two thriving monsteras in North Melbourne. He normally works in events and arts marketing (so things are pretty quiet at the moment), but also writes about movies for *Lindsay* magazine.

OVERHEAD
ELIJAH EL KAHALE

You know when you're tucked in bed, and you're processing all of your thoughts before you nod off, only to be met by one particular thought, and you're no longer able to sleep? Your eyes are heavy, but your mind and heart are racing. With this incredible mind of ours, we rehearse possible future scenarios, or just replay the past. And we love to do this so much, even when we hate it. As for these images, I wanted to convey what it must be like to be inside someone's brain, but using a different kind of scanner—an old overhead projector, where I would perform a different way to create a photogram, and all I would do then is photograph the results that came onto the wall and take it through further processing. I used old negatives that I would cut up and organise

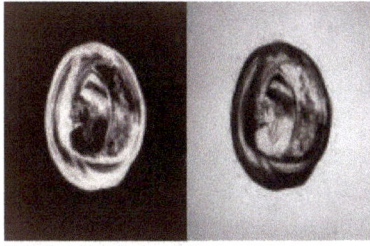

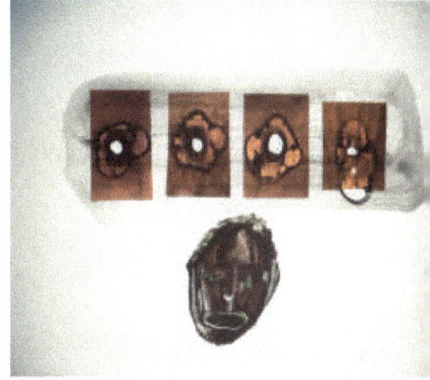

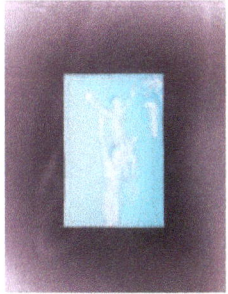

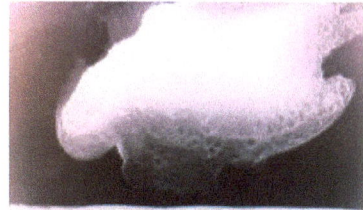

in a particular way that demonstrates the recollection of fragments. I used the thickness of the acrylic paint and the thinness of water to project colours in abstract shapes. Patterns that I don't fully control. And I would also watch the paint dry from the heat of the projector, and it reminded me of mountains, it felt like looking at a weather radar.

For me, I take those memories and construct by destroying them. Sometimes for fun, sometimes out of a sheer, intense emotion. And I deconstruct like this—scissors, paint, projector—so I don't have to ever romanticise or catastrophise, nor do I need to ever be nostalgic about a given memory again.

After all, learning yourself is the most painful thing, and in 2020 when a pandemic stopped the world, and we lost so much of what keeps us and the world alive, we took what we did every night before we fell asleep, and practiced this non-stop. Right now we are so awake as a planet, more than ever before in history, but at the cost of being deprived of not just something as healthy as resting, but of dreaming. It is one of the most vital things, and this is how I want to encourage dreaming. I can't change what happened before the camera, but I can change what happens to the memory. Unlike the camera, painting is true perception.

Raised in a Lebanese Christian family, Elijah diverted from traditions and finds solace in exploring art, fashion, music, film, culture, and philosophy. He is currently studying a Bachelor of Fine Arts.

A BOX OF UNUSED MASKS
HOLLY ZWALF

I tap on the wall and my love taps back. Like a heartbeat, like my skittish heart: so scared that I will lose him. I could text but I beat out my Morse-code message instead: I'm sorry. I love you. I'm sorry.

THUMP.

Flesh and bone against plasterboard. I withdraw my fingers and wait. My phone lights up:

he's angry he can't see you. better stop.

He, his child; trapped on the other side of the wall with my love, and another nearly ready to be born inside him. On my side of the wall my child dreams. I brush my teeth, sceptical of sleep in the half-light never-night of this room. This room which I am legally required to remain in, as I will be arrested if I attempt to leave, even if just to flick the light switch off on the wall outside the door. But surprisingly I sleep better just knowing my love is there, on the other side of my wall.

I am the 15th in Queensland. My partner is the 16th. I catch it somewhere between the UK and home. I thought I'd done the heroic thing. A missed funeral, an emergency flight, determined to get back before the birth. Heroic almost rhymes with COVID. Coming home, which is how my partner catches it: coming hard against the kitchen cupboards at home, while sleep blankets the bunkbeds in the neighbouring room. We do our best to forget the hard lump between us: hard to be a boy with such a round hard belly, but he is still hard for me.

He finds it hard to breathe at the best of times, and this is definitely the worst. My love has cystic fibrosis and now he has this; he was born with shit lungs but I've made them much worse. The doctors are scared he will die. So am I. When the ambulance is sent to collect me and my child earlier that night, to deliver us to our negative-pressure prison, I text my sister: maybe this is where I lose him. And I do. For nine long days we are held in separate rooms, while his kid quickly loses faith in the world and mine descends into endless screen time. Now is not the time to police these things, but the inert electrical hypnosis slowly gets under your skin like the grit and shame of a week-long dirty come-down. From separate rooms we hold teleconferences with medical professionals we never meet face to face. This is to be the first COVID birth outside of China, and the first non-caesarean birth to COVID-positive parents in the world, so we are making waves in the hospital that are breaking far beyond our four small walls. My love and I text, we call, we tap through the wall. His child screams for hours on end, and at the end, not that it ever really ends, I hear my love cry. I go still and cold inside like a chameleon making peace with the aircon.

Every day is a battle to get the staff to see us as people and not just as a virus. Every day is a battle to remind them we have rights. The inconsistent rules have consistently destroyed us: one child is so broken he wants to disappear, the other already has. We adults know they are one and the same. At the birth I'm not allowed to pull my mask down and kiss my partner as he sweats and groans his way through the labour, and when the baby is born I am told to wear gloves as I guide him from between my partner's legs and up onto his chest. For the last six days every touch has been muffled by gloves, and I need to feel the baby's head, the hair, the blood, the warmth. So I refuse, and then worry that I will kill him with my disease. But I need to feel something alive.

The midwives wear masks as they weigh and check and swab. My partner wears a mask to chestfeed, change a nappy, cuddle. My 4-year-old wears a mask to hold the baby. I wear a mask to hold my love. The people who nervously bring our food, who reluctantly clean our rooms, all of them wear masks. For his first week alive the baby is surrounded by strange ducks with human eyes and double-padded paper bills. He is yet to see a smile.

Our family falls apart. The kids don't understand why they can't leave, why they can't go home, why they get woken up all through the night to be hurt. The adults don't know how to make sense of it either. The baby is the only one who is ok. When we are eventually released we fall apart even more, and have to move to separate houses to finish our quarantine.

We are both still positive but we are not allowed to visit each other. We text, like most modern lovers these days. My partner sends photos and videos of the baby and I watch him get bigger through the screen. There's not much to see, but I ask for a video of him sleeping. A video of him feeding. A photo of his dirty nappy. I am missing out on so much, even the shit.

Our quarantine ends, but the distance doesn't. We stay well away from each other, far further than the regulated 1.5 metres apart. We stay 1.5 hours drive apart, a quarter of a tank each way, a full day's trip with a small child. The virus is over, but the trauma isn't; we have all learned our lesson the hard way. So we continue to stay away, the same way that people in our small regional town stay away from us on the street, the same way that parents at our kindy, and workmen with unfinished jobs, and even the GPs at the local clinic pull away in fear. I have a box of masks from our discharge from hospital that go unused. I don't know if we will ever be close enough again to need them.

Holly Zwalf is a queer solo parent by choice who lives in a little log cabin in the bush with her wild child. In her spare time, of which she has none, she is an aspiring screenwriter, smutty spoken word performer, and the coordinator of Rainbow Families Queensland.

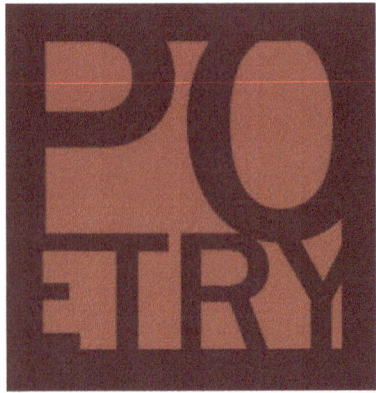

POETRY

Couch scene

CAT COTSELL

Reading together from a magazine,
my friend falls asleep with her
head
on my shoulder.
I turn the
pages so
quiet
ly.

On zoom in April we are among
the last ones left in a group chat;
her gaze drifts off
into the middle distance and
my collarbone fizzes
under a flutter of breath,
a bird's shadow landing.

Cat Cotsell is a nonbinary panromantic creative generalist. Their writing can be found in *Bent Street* volume 3, qommunicate's *Hashtag Queer* volume 2, and cicerone journal's Canberra anthology *These Strange Outcrops*. They also illustrate as Cat Hesarose.

About Me
GEORGIA BANKS

___ thirteen://

> i use the internet for the first time _ while visiting my friend]s house / we go on chat sites / she teaches me that you can lie online which i am initially surprised by / we pretend to be a seventeen year old cheerleader from somewhere in the usa // asl ? // _ which we envisage as peak sexy / we talk to men i suppose / i experience the thrill of anonymity _ and of deception

> i start talking to a girl in a chat site / she lives in america and she is blonde and very pretty and fourteen / we talk for hours / i am desperate to talk to her again the next day / we exchange emails and we email daily for months / we exchange pictures and talk about our days / it]s my first online relationship / it]s my first relationship with a girl / at some point and for some reason we cease contact

> i lose my virginity _ to a twenty seven year old while visiting a friend a few towns over / we have a sort of relationship over msn for a bit / it turns out he has a girlfriend _ who was also twenty seven or around there / she starts stalking me on msn and threatens to bash me for sleeping with her boyfriend

____ fifteen://

> a teacher shows us // the first ? // smart chat bot / we spend all afternoon trying to trick her in order to prove that she is not real _ even though we already know that she is not real

> a boy at school shows me a video of a man being beheaded

_____ sixteen://

my cousin shows me a site called vampire freaks / it]s
basically myspace for [goths] / i start my second online
relationship _ with a girl who lives in france / she sends me
emails about how her boyfriend likes her to step on his
testicles while she wears stilettos

_____ seventeen://

my boyfriend details how i had drunkenly cheated on him on
live journal and the whole school reads it

my sister and i have a party / some boys use the
computer in the lounge room to watch porn and
somehow it gets left playing all night / the next day our
dad is furious at us because of how expensive the internet bill will be

_____ eighteen://

my friend]s boyfriend uses my msn account to tell everyone
// as me // that i have a rape fantasy / i have never told him
this _ but it is true

_____ nineteen://

i join facebook. / i post my first selfie
my ex boyfriend breaks into my email account and
reads emails i have sent to another guy / after this he
won]t stop sending me abusive emails and i have to
start a new account

_____ twenty://

my sister introduces me to the concept of facebook stalking _
which i consider highly unethical

i am introduced to the website efukt, where _ among
other things _ men post videos of themselves covertly
ejaculating onto women]s backs whilst on public
transport

_____ twenty one://

my friend sends me nude images of a girl he had briefly dated / i hear that she didn]t even send them to him _ but that his friend hacked her computer and gave them to him / i hear that he sent them to a lot of people / i think this whole situation is very amusing

_____ twenty two://

two of my male friends and i like to get stoned and troll dudes on chat roulette / i]ll talk to the guy and they]ll start jerking off _ then before they cum we turn the camera around and my two friends are there smiling and giving a big thumbs up / often the guys think it]s funny but sometimes they get pretty angry / one time we get a guy to drink his own piss / one guy manages to finish before we pull the prank and i feel pretty ashamed and disgusted with myself _ but i don]t want to let on because i don]t want to bring down the mood and be [uncool]

i guess my boyfriend]s facebook password and log in to his account / i discover that he is cheating on me / when i confront him he is mad at me for invading his privacy

_____ twenty three://

after graduation my honours supervisor emails me and propositions an affair / he later says it was a joke

_____ twenty five://

i]m introduced to the red pill

i join instagram

i receive my first unsolicited dick pic

i start using tinder and okcupid / between the ages of twenty five and twenty seven i fuck approximately thirty three people from the internet

_____ twenty six://

i take naked photos of myself for 250$ _ in order to pay for
my passport / i also make a video of my face while
masturbating for a further 250$

_____ twenty eight://

i watch lots of james deen pornography / james deen is
famous for creating the best simulated rape _ bdsm _ and
torture porn / female co stars _ including one of his ex
girlfriends _ begin publicly accusing deen of sexually
assaulting them during filming / one woman says she was
afraid for her life during a shoot. / when i discover that the
[play rape] i thought i]d been watching is actual rape _ i feel
disgusted with myself / i feel sick that i have been
masturbating to women in pain _ women that are literally
afraid for their lives

james deen is [cancelled] _ and his career is declared
over

after a performance _ a man finds me on
facebook and messages me for months _ even
though i don]t respond to any of them / the last
message he sends asks _ [any huge surprises you found ?]

_____ twenty nine://

i am banned from tinder

a customer from the bar i work in finds my website and
uses it to send me messages of a sexual nature

_____ thirty://

i read that it]s been decided that james deen has been made
to suffer the consequences of his actions long enough _ and
is now allowed to make a comeback / his first comeback
feature is titled consent

i download an app that shows me when people unfollow
me on instagram / i am often surprised and hurt when
people i know unfollow me / i never confront anyone to
ask why they have unfollowed me _ but i always
unfollow them back

Georgia Banks is a current studio artist at Gertrude Contemporary, Melbourne.
She completed a Masters of Fine Arts (Research) at the Victoria College of the
Arts in 2015.

Touch
TINA HEALY

What is love without touch?

Without the lingering caress of fingers
that sing a song of grief,
a hunger,
a seaside mist, where gulls cry invisible, so lost
and miserable without your love that was gentle and blind
to my awkward kind of being, my odd way of seeing
myself …
Crazed plate on a dusty shelf …
But you loved me for who I am, your gender anagram.
I miss your touch, much as the sea misses
the sun's kisses when day powers down

What is love without touch?

I close my eyes, you rise next to me,
your love inside me, as we close the circle
to a universe space, where distance is nothing,
where love is whispered breaths of passion
moist on my breasts, and love cries as we move
as one.
I open my eyes, you are gone …
Love is a ghost, a grey dove with wings that are wraithlike,
memory fakes
that break the heart

What is love without touch?

This cursed virus that preys in silence, building walls
where loneliness falls like goodbye tears.
When your face disappears from the screen,

and I am left staring at a grey abyss …
I miss you …
No voice on a phone, or an image that beams
like a ghost in my dreams can replace
the touch of your face, the safety of
your arm's embrace
my wholeness path, my lightning and thunder
my passion that plunders an ocean of grief

What is love without touch?

Tina Healy is an advocate, peer support worker and an elder in the
transgender community. She is a dad to her children, grandma to her
grandchildren, and just 'Tina' to her community.

Offline

CASEY SCANLON

Dad
and Coronavirus
scratch in my head
at similar places
Cautious voices
Don't get close
A hug may be an act of danger
or disguised aggression

My life is on hold
Still
It's me and Dad
in a sad house.

I want a life
Outside
my bedroom
and my head
Please.

Grindr?
Okcupid?
Onlylads?

I'd rather
face-to-face
body-to-body
Passion Heat Desire Emotion
on my fingers
Because
once you hang up
you're on your own

again
Disconnected
Out of touch
Down

I want
to notice
You
over there
across a room,
even if it is only 20 people or less
and my hands smell of alcohol rub.

I am old fashioned, I explain to myself
Mostly wishing I wasn't
but
sometimes proud
of this point of difference
I'm not interested in Facebook-Fuck the phone-Fuck the people glued to
their phones-Zombies who have forgotten
to look around.

In my bedroom
I watch and wish
Friends and *I love Lucy* and *The Golden Girls*
Canned laughter is the backdrop to my 20s
But I am tough
Tougher than the smartest phone
Tough when I hit the curb

I wait to love you
Up close
offline.

Casey Scanlon has recently found his way into the gay community and is hopeful
that a relationship will follow soon. He loves animals and volunteers at the RSPCA.
The poem was developed with Henry von Doussa, who has been supporting Casey
as he finds connections in the LGBTIQ community.

King Root
BRIGITTE LEWIS

since 1983
there has been more than one way to make a connection
an intricate dance called a three-way handshake
one way to ask for permission
one way back to ensure what we have is stable
another to acknowledge our transmission
this is the language written from every keyboard that has ever called the
internet and landed on someone else's home
funny that my job title is penetration tester
not the sex kind
the ethical hacker kind
the root boxes and finger networks kind
the kind that uses language that is not kind or ethical
a reflection of a world
where master and slave are used freely
and black hats are bad and black lists are bad
and all things white are good
like white lists and white hats
and the white goods in our office kitchens
where the only kind of attack on your network is done
by a Man-in-the-Middle
and all anyone wants to do is make things fall over
and crash
so they can exploit every service you've ever stood up
to own you
with a root your mobile program called KingRoot
google it
the first response you get:
how to safely root your iphone
from oneclickroot.com

but like all things built in this world

digital or not
the voice of the Other
has always been running across the cables since the first communication
like a long held breath that meets an exhale
a Zoom call that stutters my voice as it enters your lounge room
and whispers
I don't want you to root my box without permission
like a 16 year old kid learning to hack with both their hands and their
discourse
playing out the history of oppression through ownership and submission

I want a new language to describe this position
because how do we open up this boy-in-the-hoodie world
if all the moves we see are white hands pushing on black keys tapping
white letters to create sentences only a few us fit into?
how do we move from a one way highway to new roads with new words
that are not heavy with a history built on subjugation?
we make way for neighbourhoods that house nomads looking for a new
place to rest
to wake up and resist
because the first words of the internet were not mummy or daddy but
hello world
or at least the world with the means to listen
and now we know the power of the hashtag
SOSBLAKAUSTRALIA
METOO
SAYHERNAME
BLACKLIVESMATTER

because the world wide web launched to bring us closer
but the digital divide is getting deeper
and while we mount attacks on politicians and nation states from the streets
the missiles we launch from our beds when we hold each other
the grenades we push from our hearts when we hear each other
the bullets that rain from our eyes when we see each other
these are the parts of the story that hold us together when the internet is down
and there's nothing left but to keep one fist in the air and the other re-telling stories of resistance that strut from our lips when we kiss each other.

Brigitte Lewis really does work as a penetration tester. She has written on a range of diverse topics including feminisms and feminist digital activisms, lesbian and other types of sex and desire, and cosmopolitanism. She is the author of the poetry sequence *Rubbing Mirrors*.

asleep in my arms
ROB WALLIS

asleep in my arms
he breathes
into a snuffled dream
his head a cushion
for my chin
as I lean in
smell his sweaty secrets

cuddling him
won't be enough
to save us
from this delirious world
its cankerous delusions
but when he stirs
clings tighter
our breaths eased
into breathless singularity
this intimate moment
puts the apocalypse on hold

Rob Wallis's fifth poetry collection, *Caught Jesting*, was published recently by Birdfish Books. His poems have appeared in various magazines and anthologies.

NICK'S STORY MODE
AVA REDMAN

When the university went online because of coronavirus, it wasn't the worst-case scenario, Nick thought. It took him over three hours to get to campus, travelling from the countryside to the Sydney CBD and his parents were baby boomers, closer in age to the vulnerable groups than his friends' parents were. When everything finally went online, it didn't matter. Nick had been online long before the pandemic, and now the world was simply catching up to him.

The sun broke over the trees, spearing in through the window, straight for Nick. He rolled over to the other side and blinked at his phone. He opened his messages from the night before. Alex had messaged that he missed him. He'd sent a GIF of two guys cuddling. Nick had responded by saying he missed Alex's warmth. It was as close as Nick would come to admitting he missed Alex too. Straightaway Alex messaged *ditto*, but Nick left it at that.

He hadn't seen Alex in weeks, and the last time they met, their dynamic had changed, as if coronavirus had put everything into perspective. Or at least them.

It had weighed on him, like a can of worms he hoped Alex would never open.

Nick sat up and inched out of bed. He was tall and lanky, and the cold sheeted every square inch of him as he wrapped up in multiple layers, including his blue snuggie that he preferred to wear on backwards like a wizard. He grabbed the controls from the side of his bed and sidled back in under the cover. The dogs barked below, waiting to be let out, but he ignored them. Casey would do it. He could already hear his sister in the kitchen with Dana and Michael as she probably burnt the toast and Dana wailed.

Nick pressed the remote and the TV lit up to a green pixelated field, much like the farm he lived on with his sister and her family. He checked the status of his farm, fed the chickens and checked on his family. He'd been playing house in Stardew Valley, building a farm while his wife Alexa took care of their son Nicki. It had taken some work, but Alexa had finally consented to a relationship with him after he'd given her enough salad to feed a trough of pigs. He laughed at the idea that women even liked salad. Nick tended to the farm as the sun rose higher. Occasionally his niece and nephew would scramble in and prop and poke things and then they'd leave. He couldn't understand why anyone would willingly have children. They were so curious and pointless!

Stardew Valley was a world he'd readily lost himself in during the height of the pandemic. While people were dying outside, he was building a farm that his Stardew Valley grandfather had left him, or racing through a zombie apocalypse as an 18 year old girl seeking vengeance for her father's death in *The Last of Us Part 2*. While the world cried, he cried when Kratos had finally accepted his son and had touched his shoulder to acknowledge him as heir, in *God of War*. Nick had lived and felt everything from the comfort of his chair or his bed.

His phone lit up with a message from Alex; *Hey, how's your day going?* Nick put down the controls and typed back; *Playing Stardew Valley.* Alex's reply was almost instant; *Lol.*

Alex seemed to love this part of Nick; his nerdy obsessions with video games that revolved around story mode concepts. Alex had even pointed out the irony of Nick's family life when he clearly wasn't into women, or at least didn't appear to have any interest in them besides friendship. Nick had ignored these comparisons and chose to ignore the feeling he got whenever Alex messaged him. Like he was now.

Alex shot him another message; *Say hi to the wife for me.*

Then another; *On second thoughts, better not. Don't want to get you in trouble with the missus.*

Nick picked up the phone and replied a few seconds later; *Maybe I like playing straight sometimes.*

Alex's response was almost immediate; *You like playing house, it seems.*

Nick left the message and felt the dark waters looming once again. Things were different now and Alex would want more from him soon, only Nick didn't know what to say. He still didn't trust Alex's feelings for him, how could he? Nick was a 25-year-old nerd studying IT with a penchant for video games over real human interactions and Alex was 29, hot, outspoken and opinionated, and with muscles Nick had only ever dreamed of. Their conversations were always intense, and Alex had years of wisdom from his travels abroad and a life of growing up in other countries. Nick had only moved from one part of the countryside in Bilpin, to down the road into his sisters' place.

Another message popped up on his screen; *I feel like you're avoiding me.*

Nick glanced at it, sighed, and fed his pixelated chickens.

Another message buzzed on his phone.

I think we need to talk, at least.

Nick put down the controls and stared at the phone.

Instead he went into the kitchen and grabbed a chocolate chip muffin from the counter, patting Dana on the head who lolled her tongue out playing puppy and pushing Michael off who tried to lick his arm.

When he returned there were multiple messages from Alex. Instead he opened the message that had come ten minutes ago from his childhood best friend, Brendan. His *straight* friend.

Hey poofta. How's it hangin.

Nick responded with; *Not much, faggot.*

Nick and Brendan had talked like this for years, long before Nick knew of a closet, that he was in one; or that he was meant to come out of one eventually. But Brendan had been there for all of it with his butt-licking, butt-plugging, faggot-fisting jokes. Even when Nick hadn't known, Brendan had suspected; still they'd been friends since they could remember.

Brendan's reply came a minute later; *Sorry, I mean, how are you? What have you been up to?*

Nick snickered and replied with; *Is Emma looking over your shoulder again?*

His friend's response was immediate; *She thinks I don't talk to you in the 'politically correct way'.*

Nick wrote back; *What's the point of having a token gay friend if you can't have a faggot riff-off?*

Brendan messaged back; *There's fumes coming out of her ears!*

Nick beamed and wrote back; *Did you tell her you were the one who forced me to go to PoofDoof at Ivy and to Arq and Stonewall? I wouldn't be the gay I am now if it weren't for you.*

Nick almost laughed knowing he wasn't the gay anyone had expected. He certainly didn't possess the feminine skills that made him lovable to women like a collectable limited-edition barbie doll. His sisters had been mildly disappointed, and his mother still tried to get him to take an interest in her arts and crafts.

Brendan messaged a minute later; *I'm such a giver!*

Nick knew Emma would be looking over Brendan's shoulder at their messages, probably beaming that her fiancé was so forward thinking, but it would be a while before Nick and Emma went shopping together. Nick wasn't cut out for this stereotype just yet.

He opened up his messages from Alex.

Hey, I don't want to scare you off. I just want you to know I have feelings for you, and I was hoping you did too. I'm not expecting anything from you, but I get this vibe that we work well together.

We're good at being apart and we're amazing when we're together.

I just thought you should know because you're acting weird and how can I not notice that?

I miss you.

Nick hugged his knees close to his chest, as the messages filled him with a feeling that he didn't want to describe, didn't want to acknowledge. He wanted Alex. But it was all too fast. Too soon.

He started typing the words, typing something, anything to make it all ok. He imagined Alex on the other end, watching, waiting. He pressed delete and picked up his remote and played house with Alexa and his son.

Ava Redman's writing has been published in *Verge*, *City Hub* and *W'Sup* online. She is currently majoring in journalism at Western Sydney City Campus.

PATCHOULI
HEATH JOHN RAMSAY

I was particularly nervous about my date with Jeremy as in the short time I'd known him I'd already assessed that he was a much better vegan than I was.

Jeremy was spiritual, political and evolved and seemed to glisten whenever I saw him. He'd been a vegan since the age of fourteen and had participated in fortnightly colonic irrigation treatments since his twenty-first birthday. Suffice it to say, and Jeremy often would, his body was officially free of rotting meat.

I was new to being vegan and remained very private about the fact that my choice was entirely based on an inebriated, late-night Google search as to how Anne Hathaway had dropped twelve kilos to play Fantine in *Les Miserable*.

I was desperate to lose weight for my upcoming audition for 'Married at First Sight' and had zero interest in gradual, safe weight loss. Adopting a plant-based diet with 'negative gearing' seemed the very best place to start. Inspired by Anne's commitment and gritty determination (to win an Oscar), I began to eat one small bowl of oats a day, covered with boiling water and accompanied with no more than four cups of stinging nettle tea. Three days in, feeling constantly weak and plagued by chronic diarrhoea, I knew I'd found a program that would deliver results.

With my hot date less than four hours away, I began my ascension from nervous to excited, bolstered as I was from an afternoon of napping (fainting) and ruminating on reflections and insights from sessions with my former life coach, Barry Pam. I'd also started mixing Absolut Vodka with my nettle tea, initiating my 'pre-emptive strike' protocol where alcohol followed by an appropriately timed Xanax chaser would dissolve the granite walls of my cool exterior, thus revealing a far more gregarious and indiscriminate 'party guy' who'd grown quite fond of impromptu, unsolicited performances of the Beach Boys classic hit *Kokomo*, a song I over appreciate for its heady mix of tropical pop eroticism

I poured my first *Stinger* at 3:00 and grabbed my *Just Do It Journal* to channel the inimitable wisdom of Barry Pam, who I hoped would serve as a spiritual guide for tonight's proceedings. Upon flicking open the cover I was immediately teleported back to our first session and could literally smell the distinct blend of black coffee and mild sedatives on his breath. I carefully selected several pertinent Barry quotes and wrote them on my wall in permanent marker:

By failing to prepare you are preparing to fail

Don't expect success, prepare for it

People who want to appear clever rely on memory. People who want to get things done make lists

and my personal favourite:

Take the t out of can't and you can

Barry and I had maintained a special bond until I revealed just enough of my private inner self to frighten him off. Heaven forbid I divulge my secret affliction, a uniquely violent type of vertigo wherein I honestly feel compelled (and then have to resist) pushing people in front of trains. Wow, Barry, how very empathetic of you, perhaps you shouldn't work so hard on establishing trust if you're not willing to navigate the rewards.

Shoving my feelings of mild contempt for Barry into my hurt locker, I began my research into the presentational elements of the night ahead. This involved trawling through a series of dubious websites until I happened upon the aptly titled *Gay Vegan Hippie Tumblr*. What a revelation! I was so excited by my discovery I instantly rewarded myself with a double stinger. Laptop in hand, I opened my desktop folder VISION BOARD and commenced the rather titillating task of drag-and-dropping images of scantily clad, dreadlocked, nubile men, admirable for their ability to realise the perfect balance between grimy and clean. As a seemingly endless glut of hippie smut populated my folder, I continually fought the urge to gently masturbate.

Vision board complete, it was time for one more stinger and a much-needed foray into Barry Pam's *Free Your Mind and the Rest Will Follow— Vision Board Embodiment Technique*. This was a wildly energetic and frenzied up-tempo meditation which required the participant to dance fully naked whilst honouring and anointing themselves in the mirror as they 'made space' for their new identity. I set my vision board folder to slideshow and immediately disrobed. As the sounds of tropical pop eroticism swelled to fill the room, I became dizzy with the promise of enlightenment, or perhaps it was due to malnutrition. I grabbed my triple vodka stinger and attempted to time my sips with the flick of a new image, audibly digesting my new self with loud gulps.

'BARRY, YOU'RE A DISLOYAL GENIUS' I exclaimed as I rubbed organic extra-virgin coconut oil over my entire body. I was now on an almost natural high (leaving aside my imbibing half a bottle of vodka) and was feeling unreservedly ready to create my list.

Hair—tousled and knotted, spritzed with a mist of olive oil cooking spray, to be twisted and played with in accordance to the varying intensity of our conversation

Face—fresh, clean, powdered (not noticeably, just enough to cover my coconut slick) winsome facial expressions to be favoured: contemplative, bemused, intolerant, dangerous, kind

Outfit—Rainbow Cyclone Tie-Dye Baja Hoodie, Grateful Dead— Steal Your Face Cargo Pants

NO UNDERWEAR OR SHOES

Jewellery—Oil Diffuser Locket Necklace, Imagine Stretch Bracelet, Jingle Bell Anklet Bracelet, In The Mood Ring, ideally with colour settling on 'aroused'

Scent—A patchouli, sandalwood combo—hints of musk—homemade bicarb soda paste deodorant applied liberally to armpits

Smugly over satisfied with what was arguably one of the world's best lists, I ceremoniously adorned my shiny self with the regalia of the new me. Standing before the mirror, I made one minor inspired adjustment (I rubbed some activated charcoal into my knuckles to promote an earthier look) before finishing the bottle of Absolut …

Dear Reader, I think by this point we've established a climate wherein my being completely candid is not only appropriate but rather endearing and utterly compelling, perhaps the tipping point was when I shared my struggle to not masturbate whilst leering at *Gay Vegan Hippie Tumblr*. Regardless of said tipping point, I feel completely safe to share with you just how attractive I found the glorious reflection of myself contained within my decorative acrylic mirror. Upon first glance I quickly yelled out 'HOT DAMN' followed by 'CRIKEY' and then 'BAM'. I involuntarily slipped my hand beneath the elastic waistband of my Grateful Dead Steal Your Face Cargo Pants, to give my penis a congratulatory tug. If the combination of my exquisite appearance and the antics of those displayed on *Gay Vegan Hippie Tumblr* were anything to go by, a certain someone was set to be involved in what the new me would like to term 'a sacred sacral chakra shakeout'.

After a considerable amount of time swimming in the dazzling display of my reflection, it was only the sound of my 'time for Xanax' alarm that was able to break through my reverie. I briefly considered cancelling my date altogether to allow for a much deeper personal adulation session, but the thought occurred to me that sexual gratification was often best experienced with at least one other person. With that in mind, I quickly popped a Xanax and daubed a small amount of patchouli directly onto my pubis, a level of commitment I'm sure Anne Hathaway would champion.

I swiftly grabbed a final prop, my Peace Fringe Leather Shoulder Bag and made for the door. Galvanised by the slight burning pain of having applied an undiluted essential oil to my crotch, I remembered another quote from Barry; 'If it hurts it's helping'.

In a state of sheer bliss, I sashayed towards the train station and certain victory.

Heath John Ramsay, actor, sub-average singer, private dancer, pop culture glutton, former colourist at *Elevation Hair & Beauty* and Enrolments Advisor at *The Phoenix Institute* (raided by the Federal Police in March 2016) can now add 'writer' to his short list of accomplishments.